Questions

People and Churches Ask

Charles Brock

Copyright 1988 Charles Brock

Published by
Church Growth International
13174 Owens Lane
Neosho, Missouri 64850

All rights reserved. No portion of this book may be reproduced in any way without the written permission of the publisher, with the exception of brief excerpts quoted in magazine reviews, etc.

Scripture references are from *Today's English Version* unless otherwise stated.

ISBN 1-885504-43-8

With Gratitude, Dottie and I dedicate this book to

J O and Velma Brock
Jesse and Twyla Richardson

Our parents who loved God and their children.

Contents

                                                                                           Page

Questions People Ask:

1. Is the Bible the final authority for the Christian? 7
2. Why should I study the Bible? 11
3. How should I study the Bible? 16
4. Do all roads lead to heaven? 19
5. Is it true that a person must be born again to go to heaven? 22
6. What must a person do to be born again? 24
7. How will I respond to those who oppose my decision if I am born again? 30
8. May I continue to go to my church if I am born again? 33
9. Who should I follow? 35
10. What about the funeral and burial services if I enter a new religion? 39
11. Why do I need to be baptized again? 43
12. Who are Baptists? 47
13. Did Mary continue to be a virgin after the birth of Jesus? 53
14. What is Christian prayer? 57
15. Should I use the rosary in prayer? 61
16. What does the Bible teach about images or idols? 64
17. What does the Bible teach about purgatory and praying for the dead? 67
18. Do I need to fear evil spirits after I am born again? 71
19. Should I have my baby baptized? 78
20. What about the salvation of children? 82
21. Can I lose my salvation after I am born again? 88
22. Should I tithe? 91
23. What does the Bible teach about communion? 96
24. What does the Bible teach concerning homosexuality? 99
25. Is it wrong to drink alcoholic beverages and smoke cigarettes? . 104
26. What does the Bible say about speaking in unknown tongues? . 109
27. What am I to do when someone wrongs me? 115
28. What is a Christian marriage? 121
29. How am I to discipline my children? 128
30. What titles do we use when referring to religious leaders? 132

Questions Churches Ask:

31. What is a church? 136
32. What is a healthy indigenous church? 143
33. Who is the head of the church? 148
34. How should a church business meeting be conducted? 150
35. What are the qualifications and responsibilities of a church treasurer? 154
36. What are the qualifications and responsibilities of a church secretary? 157
37. What are the qualifications for a pastor? 159
38. How does a church get a pastor? 163
39. Should our pastor be ordained? 168
40. Should a pastor have an outside job? 175
41. How do I prepare a sermon? 177
42. How should an invitation be given? 181
43. What are the roles of the pastor and the members of the church? 187
44. What does the Bible say about deacons? 193
45. Who should be allowed to speak to the church? 198
46. How does a church receive new members? 200
47. How should a baptismal service be conducted? 203
48. How does a church observe the Lord's Supper? 206
49. How should a dedication service for a child be conducted? ... 211
50. What should we do when there is an emergency need in one of the church families? 216
51. How does a church discipline members? 220
52. How can a church encourage members to study the Bible? 227

PREFACE

Questions People and Churches Ask was written after years of church planting in the United States and the Philippines. This edition has been edited for broader usage around the world. It is not intended to be an exhaustive theological, philosophical approach. The book is designed to help the new pastor of a new church in the bush of Africa or an untrained pastor of a new church in Los Angeles. Many of the questions are answered directly from the Bible. I believe what the Bible says is more important and more powerful than anything anyone could say about the Bible, therefore the Bible is trusted to speak. The answers are brief and easy to understand.

Most of the questions are those I was asked in my more than 26 years of church planting in the United States and in the Philippines. A few of the questions are ones I personally feel need to be dealt with in every congregation.

This should be of special value as a guide and resource book for new church members and newly planted churches. It has proven to be very acceptable for basic leadership training.

My prayer is that it can be used for God's glory.

A special word of appreciation to my wife Dottie who is my co-laborer in the Gospel Ministry. Her encouragement and love can be measured only in eternity. She has been the chief editor for this book as well as for all others that I have written.

1997

Charles Brock

Chapter 1

IS THE BIBLE THE FINAL AUTHORITY FOR THE CHRISTIAN?

Can the Bible be trusted? Is it reliable? Is it God's Word? If it is God's Word, should church leaders alter or replace it with their words?

What does the Bible say concerning the Holy Scriptures?

...ever since you were a child, you have known the Holy Scriptures, which are able to give you the wisdom that leads to salvation through faith in Christ Jesus. All Scripture is inspired by God and is useful for teaching the truth, rebuking error, correcting faults, and giving instruction for right living, so that the person who serves God may be fully qualified and equipped to do every kind of good deed. 2 Timothy 3:15-17

For no prophetic message ever came just from the will of man, but men were under the control of the Holy Spirit as they spoke the message that came from God. 2 Peter 1:21

The word of God is alive and active, sharper than any double-edged sword. It cuts all the way through, to where soul and spirit meet, to where joints and marrow come together. It judges the desires and thoughts of man's heart. Hebrews 4:12

In the Old Testament we read, *Your Word, O Lord, will last forever; it is eternal in heaven.* Psalm 119:89

Your word is a lamp to guide me and a light for my path. Psalm 119:105

Jesus said, *"Do not think that I have come to do away with the Law of Moses and the teachings of the prophets. I have not come to do away with them, but to make their teachings come true. Remember that as long as heaven and earth last, not the least point nor the smallest detail of the Law will be done away with—not until the end of all things."* Matthew 5:17-18

Paul said, *I have complete confidence in the gospel; it is God's power to save all who believe, first the Jews and also the Gentiles. For the gospel reveals how God puts people right with himself: it is through faith from beginning to end. As the scripture says, "The person who is put right with God through faith shall live."* Romans 1:16-17

Jesus Christ accepted the Scriptures as the Word of God.

When facing the temptations from Satan, Jesus quoted scripture from the Old Testament when he said, *...man must not depend on bread alone to sustain him, but on everything that the Lord says.* Deuteronomy 8:3

Jesus answered them, "How wrong you are! It is because you don't know the Scriptures or God's power." Matthew 22:29

"If you had really believed Moses, you would have believed me, because he wrote about me. But since you do not believe what he wrote, how can you believe what I say?" John 5:46-47

Then Jesus went to Nazareth, where he had been brought up, and on the Sabbath he went as usual to the synagogue. He stood up to read the Scriptures and was handed the book of the prophet Isaiah. He unrolled the scroll and found the place where it is written... Luke 4:16-17

There are many who respect the Bible, yet do not follow it as the final authority.

Paul spoke of such people when he said, *We are not like so many others, who handle God's message as if it were cheap merchandise; but because God has sent us, we speak with sincerity in his presence, as servants of Christ.* 2 Corinthians 2:17

In Mark 7:6-9, Jesus describes sincere religious leaders walking in darkness. *Jesus answered them, "How right Isaiah was when he prophesied about you! You are hypocrites, just as he wrote: 'These people, says God, honor me with their words, but their heart is really far away from me. It is no use for them to worship me, because they teach man-made rules as though they were my laws!' "You put aside God's command and obey the teachings of men." And Jesus continued, "You have a clever way of rejecting God's law in order to uphold your own teaching."*

Jesus was talking to religious authorities in John 5:37-40 when he said, *"And the Father, who sent me, also testifies on my behalf. You have never heard his voice or seen his face, and you do not keep his message in your hearts, for you do not believe in the one whom he sent. You study the Scriptures because you think that in them you will find eternal life. And these very Scriptures speak about me! Yet you are not willing to come to me in order to have life."*

The Danger of Adding to or Taking Away from the Bible.

Do not add anything to what I command you, and do not take anything away. Deuteronomy 4:2

But even if we or an angel from heaven should preach to you a gospel that is different from the one we preached to you, may he be condemned to hell! We have said it before, and now I say it again: if anyone preaches to you a gospel that is different from the one you accepted, may he be condemned to hell! Galatians 1:8-9

I, John, solemnly warn everyone who hears the prophetic words of this book: if anyone adds anything to them, God will add to his punishment the plagues described in this book. And if anyone takes anything away from the prophetic words of this book, God will take away from him his share of the fruit of the tree of life and of the Holy City, which are described in this book. Revelation 22:18-19

Conclusion:

1. The Bible is sufficient. It gives a full view of the way of salvation.

2. The Bible is complete in its message on how to live.

3. The Bible is the inspired Word of God.

4. Since the Bible is inspired, it should be accepted as it is, without change.

5. Religious leaders who add to or take away from the Bible's message are not from God and they face eternal judgment.

6. Beware of any religious group that adds to the Bible.

7. Because the Bible is the Word of God, the believer will desire to learn its contents and apply the teachings to his life.

8. If there are doctrines that you cling to but which are not found in the Bible, you need to examine your religion. Perhaps you are being led astray by religious authorities. Only God's Word is God's Word.

Chapter 2

WHY SHOULD I STUDY THE BIBLE?

1. I should study the Bible because I want to know the truth.

Man must have some standard by which to determine what is truth. For some people this standard is the ever changing words of religious leaders. This is a very dangerous and unreliable standard because, according to the Bible and according to observation, all men and women are sinners. No person who believes and takes the Bible seriously will allow any human personality to be the ultimate religious authority in his life. The world is filled with people who have been deceived and blinded by sincere, yet blind leaders. Jesus spoke of this in Luke 11:52, *"How terrible for you teachers of the Law! You have kept the key that opens the door to the house of knowledge; you yourselves will not go in, and you stop those who are trying to go in!"*

Can the Bible be trusted as my authority? Is the Bible greater than the words of men on earth today? If the Bible teaches one thing and my religion teaches another, which is right? What can I follow as my standard of authority? Note what the Bible says:

But as for you, continue in the truths that you were taught and firmly believe. You know who your teachers were, and you remember that ever since you were a child you have known the Holy Scriptures, which are able to give you the wisdom that leads to salvation through faith in Christ Jesus. All Scripture is inspired by God and is useful for teaching the truth, rebuking error, correcting faults, and giving instruction for right living, so that the person who serves God may be fully qualified and equipped to do every kind of good deed. 2 Timothy 3:14-17

In 1 Peter 1:24-25 we read: *As the Scripture says, "All mankind are like grass, and all their glory is like wild flowers. The grass withers, and flowers fall, but the word of the Lord remains forever."* In these verses "all mankind" is compared with the Word of God. Every religious leader is going to wither and fall, but the Word of God will stand for eternity. Which can a person rely upon? The words of man or the Word of God?

Concerning the reliability of the Scripture, Peter says, *For no prophetic message ever came just from the will of man, but men were under the control of the Holy Spirit as they spoke the message that came from God.* 2 Peter 1:21

Paul used the Scriptures as a basis for his teachings. *According to his usual habit Paul went to the synagogue. There during three Sabbaths he held discussions with the people, quoting and explaining the Scriptures, and proving from them that the Messiah had to suffer and rise from death.* Acts 17:2-3

Note some basic truths seen in these verses. Paul's book of authority was the Word of God. He used the Scriptures to prove a fact. He believed the Scriptures to be a trustworthy authority. Paul's subject was Jesus, His death and resurrection. Here, as always in the Bible, Christ is the key figure. Only when religious leaders deny the Bible as final and ultimate authority do you find personalities other than Christ magnified and glorified.

In Acts we read, *When they arrived, they went to the synagogue. The people there were more open-minded than the people in Thessalonica. They listened to the message with great eagerness, and every day they studied the Scriptures to see if what Paul said was really true. Many of them believed;...* Acts 17:10-12a

How does a person know what is true? Read the above verses again and you will see that we should compare the words of religious leaders with the Word of God. If they are the same, the truth has been found and you can trust that religious leader. One should never accept words of men without being sure their words are based clearly upon the Bible.

Why should I study the Bible? Eternity is too long for me and my children to make a mistake about truth. I don't want to be wrong. Jesus said, *"How wrong you are! It is because you don't know the Scriptures or God's power."* Matthew 22:29

Jesus said in His prayer to His Father, *"Your Word is truth."* John 17:17

2. I study the Bible to learn about Jesus.

In the Scriptures Jesus claimed to be one with the Father. *"The Father and I are one."* John 10:30

In the Scriptures He claimed to be the only way to the Father and the only way to heaven. *Jesus answered him, "I am the way, the truth, and the life; no one goes to the Father except by me."* John 14:6

In the Scriptures Jesus claimed to have final authority. *Jesus drew near and said to them, "I have been given all authority in heaven and on earth."* Matthew 28:18

In the Scriptures Jesus demands the allegiance of those who desire to know a life of peace and freedom. *So Jesus said to those who believed in him, "If you obey my teaching, you are really my disciples: you will know the truth, and the truth will set you free."* John 8:31-32

3. I study the Bible to learn how to receive eternal life.

Only in the Scriptures do we find the Christian view of true salvation. I must study the Bible to see if what I have been taught is in harmony with the Bible. Life after death is a serious matter. The Bible is very clear and emphatic about the way of salvation.

Paul said, *I have complete confidence in the gospel; it is God's power to save all who believe, first the Jews and also the Gentiles. For the gospel reveals how God puts people right with himself: it is through faith from beginning to end. As the Scripture says, "The person who is put right with God through faith shall live."* Romans 1:16-17

...you have known the Holy Scriptures, which are able to give you the wisdom that leads to salvation through faith in Christ Jesus. 2 Timothy 3:15

God's Word is clear, *God puts people right through their faith in Jesus Christ. God does this to all who believe in Christ, because there is no difference at all: everyone has sinned and is far away from God's saving presence. But by the free gift of God's grace all are put right with him through Christ Jesus, who sets them free.* Romans 3:22-24

4. I study the Bible because I want to live a victorious and meaningful life.

The Bible says, *All Scripture is inspired by God and is useful for teaching the truth, rebuking error, correcting faults, and giving instruction for right living...* 2 Timothy 3:16

Peter speaks of a meaningful and victorious life: *But you are the chosen race, the King's priests, the holy nation, God's own people, chosen to proclaim the wonderful acts of God, who called you out of darkness into his own marvelous light. At one time you were not God's people, but now you are his people; at one time you did not know God's mercy, but now you have received his mercy.* 1 Peter 2:9-10

David gives us a picture of victory and purpose in Psalms 40:1-4, *I waited patiently for the Lord's help; then he listened to me and heard my cry. He pulled me out of a dangerous pit, out of the deadly quicksand. He set me safely on a rock and made me secure. He taught me to sing a new song, a song of praise to our God. Many who see this will take warning and will put their trust in the Lord. Happy are those who trust the Lord...*

These verses give a picture of deliverance from destruction, a new life of victory. It is a life of purpose worth sharing with others. The Bible is the road map to successful living. The study of the Bible is the best education available on how to live victoriously. To have all human knowledge and not know the contents of the Book of Books is shortsighted foolishness.

In order to know God, to know the truth, to know the way of salvation, to know a victorious and meaningful life, I must study the Bible.

Chapter 3

HOW SHOULD I STUDY THE BIBLE?

1. Get a good quality Bible.
   Some things to look for when buying a Bible are:
   Durable materials.
   Easy to read print.
   Wide margins for placing cross references and notes.
   Translation that is easy for you to read and understand.

2. Purchase a notebook about the same size as your Bible.

3. Purchase a box of crayons and a good fine point pen.
   Take the yellow, pink, yellow green, and yellow orange crayons from the box. (Yellow is the best to use for most highlighting. Do not use dark colors.) These are good for highlighting verses that stand out to you. They do not bleed through or smear on the paper. (Be careful that in your excitement you do not mark everything you read.)

   You will use the pen to underline key verses and to write in the margins of the Bible.

4. Determine that you are going to give a part of each day to Bible study.

   If you don't think you have time, think of the time you use in reading other materials, watching television, listening to the radio, talking with people, and eating. Reading God's Word is more important than any of these.

5. Choose the study time that is best for you. For some it will be late at night, for some it will be in the afternoon and for others it may be in the early morning hours.

6. If possible read more than a chapter a day. It is like receiving a five page letter from a dear friend and reading a page a day until all of the letter is read after five days. It is less meaningful when read like this.

7. Set a goal to read a minimum of three chapters every day. If you read three chapters every day, you will read the entire Bible in a year.

8. Start with any book you want to read. It is not necessary to start on the first page of the Bible. If you are not very familiar with the Bible, it may be best to major on New Testament books at first, perhaps reading John or one of the other Gospels, then Acts, then continuing with the Epistles (books following Acts). The New Testament is the foundation for the Christian life, but it is important that you read the Old Testament also. The Old Testament shows God's working throughout the history of mankind and is the foundation for the New Testament.

9. Start at the first chapter of the book you choose and read it all the way through. Each book has a theme and normally it is best to read all of the book before going to another book.

10. You should keep a daily record of what you read—the source (book of the Bible) and the number of chapters. This can be done on a calendar or in a diary.

11. You will want to make some notes in the notebook. Write the key topics and the references. (A reference is book, chapter and verse.)

17

12. Total the chapters read during the week and record the number at the end of the week.

13. In the notebook write down some of the great truths you have learned in the week's reading. Note verses that especially spoke to your heart.

14. When you have finished reading all of the Bible, start over again. Determine to read all of the Bible at least once each year. You can read the Bible through every year for a life time and still find new truths every time you read it.

15. There will be times when you will want to give special attention to a certain topic or a chapter for in-depth study. This should be done in addition to your regular Bible reading program.

Chapter 4

DO ALL ROADS LEAD TO HEAVEN?

Some people say, "We are all going to heaven, but on different roads." Is this a true statement? What does the Bible say about it?

Speaking of Jesus, Peter said, *"Salvation is to be found through him alone; in all the world there is no one else whom God has given who can save us."* Acts 4:12

I am writing this to you, my children, so that you will not sin; but if anyone does sin, we have someone who pleads with the Father on our behalf—Jesus Christ, the righteous one. And Christ himself is the means by which our sins are forgiven, and not our sins only, but also the sins of everyone. 1 John 2:1-2

Paul said, *For it was by God's own decision that the Son has in himself the full nature of God. Through the Son, then, God decided to bring the whole universe back to himself. God made peace through his Son's death on the cross and so brought back to himself all things, both on earth and in heaven.* Colossians 1:19-20

Concerning the idea that salvation comes through keeping the law, Paul said, *Yet we know that a person is put right with God only through faith in Jesus Christ, never by doing what the Law requires. We, too, have believed in Christ Jesus in order to be put right with God through our faith in Christ, and not by doing what the Law requires. For no one is put right with God by doing what the Law requires.* Galatians 2:16

In 2 Corinthians 5:17-19, Paul says, *When anyone is joined to Christ, he is a new being; the old is gone, the new has come. All this is done by God, who through Christ changed us from enemies into his friends and gave us the task of making others his friends also. Our message is that God was making all mankind his friends through Christ.*

Paul said, *What an unhappy man I am! Who will rescue me from this body that is taking me to death? Thanks be to God, who does this through our Lord Jesus Christ!* Romans 7:24-25

In Romans 5:1 the Bible says, *Now that we have been put right with God through faith, we have peace with God through our Lord Jesus Christ.*

In Romans 3:21-24 we read, *But now God's way of putting people right with himself has been revealed. It has nothing to do with law, ...God puts people right through their faith in Jesus Christ. God does this to all who believe in Christ, because there is no difference at all: everyone has sinned and is far away from God's saving presence. But by the free gift of God's grace all are put right with him through Christ Jesus, who sets them free.*

Jesus said, *"I am the way, the truth, and the life; no one goes to the Father except by me."* John 14:6

In John 5:26 we read, *Just as the Father is himself the source of life, in the same way he has made his Son to be the source of life.*

In John 3:18 we read, *Whoever believes in the Son is not judged; but whoever does not believe has already been judged, because he has not believed in God's only Son.*

Jesus said, *"I am telling you the truth; no one can see the Kingdom of God unless he is born again."* John 3:3

Based upon these verses from the Bible the message is clear:

There is only one source of eternal life—Jesus Christ. No other name is given except Jesus. There is no mention of anyone who helps Jesus in bringing salvation to man. It is Jesus plus no one. (Acts 4:12, paragraph two of this lesson)

Christ is received by faith. (Galatians 2:16)

Some will receive Christ as their personal Savior and Lord while others will decide not to receive Him. Eternal life is the future for those who receive Him by faith; eternal punishment awaits those who decide not to follow Him. (John 3:18)

There is no salvation in keeping laws, rules, or rituals of any church or religion. (Galatians 2:16)

There is one plan for the salvation of people and it comes from God. No religion can change God's plan. (Romans 3:21-24)

Only those who follow God's plan will have a meaningful life here and life in heaven. Only a minority will go to heaven. (Matthew 7:13-14, below)

The statement, "All roads lead to heaven," is false.

In Matthew 7:13-14 Jesus said, *"Go in through the narrow gate, because the gate to hell is wide and the road that leads to it is easy, and there are many who travel it. But the gate to life is narrow and the way that leads to it is hard, and there are few people who find it."*

(Note: there is only one gate.)

Chapter 5

IS IT TRUE THAT A PERSON MUST BE BORN AGAIN IN ORDER TO GO TO HEAVEN?

The answer is very clear. Jesus Christ said, *"I am telling you the truth; no one can see the Kingdom of God unless he is born again."* John 3:3

The answer of Jesus is that no one can go to heaven or see the Kingdom of God unless he is born again. "No one" includes all people. If a person can go to heaven without being born again, then Jesus is a liar. A person may respond, "But I go to church. Do you mean I cannot go to heaven if I am not born again?" You are right; that is what Jesus said.

A person may respond, "But is that fair? Will God send a person to hell just because he has not been born again?"

God is not willing that anyone go to hell, but He will not force a person to be obedient to His commands. People have the opportunity to hear the good news and if they choose to follow their religion rather than the Bible and Christ, they are the ones choosing where they will spend eternity.

A person may respond, "But I don't know what it means to be born again. Does it still mean that I will not go to heaven?" When Jesus said "no one," He meant all who are not born again. It means those who are wealthy, poor, educated, uneducated, the religious and unreligious. It includes all. The fact that you have not been taught the importance and the way of being born again does not excuse you. You are responsible for who you follow.

Jesus told Nicodemus that he must be born again. Nicodemus was a very religious man, even a leader in his religion. Yet Jesus said to him, "Unless you are born again, you cannot see the Kingdom of God." So to the church member and to the religious leader, the words of Christ apply. To all religious groups, the message is the same. If a person does not clearly understand what it means to be born again, he needs to look for a religious group that teaches the Bible as the absolute authority.

The new birth is not optional. Jesus repeated in John 3:7, *"Do not be surprised because I tell you that you must all be born again."*

Chapter 6

WHAT MUST A PERSON DO TO BE BORN AGAIN?

The words "born again" are found in John 3. Jesus said to Nicodemus, who was a religious leader, *"Unless a person is born again he cannot see the Kingdom of God."* John 3:3

The term "born again" is not used often in the New Testament, but there are other words which describe a person's relationship with God and they speak of the same experience. They all are talking about the gift of salvation that comes from God to man.

Saved

In Acts 16:29-30 we find words which mean the same as "What must I do to be born again?" *The jailer called for a light, rushed in, and fell trembling at the feet of Paul and Silas. Then he led them out and asked, "Sirs, what must I do to be saved?"* On another occasion Jesus said, *"The Son of Man came to seek and to save the lost."* Luke 19:10

Receive Eternal Life

In Mark 10:17 we read, *As Jesus was starting on his way again, a man ran up, knelt before him, and asked him, "Good Teacher, what must I do to receive eternal life?"* In John 3:36 Jesus said, "Whoever believes in the Son has eternal life."

Put Right with God

For we conclude that a person is put right with God only through faith, and not by doing what the Law commands. Romans 3:28

Also in Romans 1:17, *For the gospel reveals how God puts people right with himself: it is through faith from beginning to end.*

A Christian is someone who has:
    been born again;
    been put right with God;
    received eternal life;
    been saved.
All of these refer to the salvation experience.

So back to the original question, "What must I do to be born again?" The answer is the same as for "What must I do to be saved?" or "What must I do to be put right with God?" or "What must I do to receive eternal life?"

ACCORDING TO THE BIBLE, What must a person do to have eternal life or be born again?

1. Hear the Good News

The Bible says, *But how can they call to him for help if they have not believed? And how can they believe if they have not heard the message? ...So then, faith comes from hearing the message, and the message comes through preaching Christ.* Romans 10:14,17

2. Repent of Sin

Jesus said, *"The right time has come and the Kingdom of God is near! Turn away from your sins and believe the Good News!"* Mark 1:15

In 1 John 1:19, we read, *But if we confess our sins to God, he will keep his promise and do what is right: he will forgive us our sins and purify us from all our wrongdoing.*

To repent means to turn away from sin. Before a person can repent of sin he must know what the sin is that condemns him or separates him from God. John 3:18 helps us understand the sin that is forever fatal unless repented of. *Whoever believes in the Son is not judged; but whoever does not believe has already been judged, because he has not believed in God's only son.* This verse clearly states that a person is judged, or condemned, **because of unbelief**. Sin is rejecting Jesus Christ as personal Savior and Lord. Many religious people respect and believe about Christ, but have failed to rely one hundred per cent upon Him for salvation. They accept additional doctrines related to salvation which are not in the Bible. These people carry the name Christian but are not true Christians. The sin of a self-righteous self-rule must be repented of.

3. Receive Jesus Christ as Savior and Lord

The Bible says, *Some, however, did receive him and believed in him; so he gave them the right to become God's children.* John 1:12

You will note in this verse the use of two words to describe the same experience, **receive** and **believe**.

How can a person receive? It is through believing. Believing is faith. Before a person can receive Christ as his Savior and Lord, he must believe that Christ is who He claims to be (Son of God) and can do what He claims He can do (give eternal life). Christ is received through faith. Faith that brings salvation must be in Christ—not in Christ plus someone else or something else. Salvation can never come through a combination of faith in Christ and good works or rituals of a church. It is faith in Christ alone that brings a person into a right relationship with God.

Note the following verses from the Bible.

For God loved the world so much that he gave his only Son, so that everyone who believes in him may not die but have eternal life. For God did not send his Son into the world to be its judge, but to be its savior. John 3:16-17

I am telling you the truth: whoever hears my words and believes in him who sent me has eternal life. He will not be judged, but has already passed from death to life. John 5:24

Jesus said to her, "I am the resurrection and the life. Whoever believes in me will live, even though he dies; and whoever lives and believes in me will never die." John 11:25-26

Jesus answered him, "I am the way, the truth, and the life; no one goes to the Father except by me." John 14:6

Salvation is to be found through him alone; in all the world there is no one else whom God has given who can save us. Acts 4:12

The gospel reveals how God puts people right with himself: it is through faith from beginning to end. Romans 1:17

Now that we have been put right with God through faith, we have peace with God through our Lord Jesus Christ. Romans 5:1

For it is by our faith that we are put right with God. Romans 10:10

Yet we know that a person is put right with God only through faith in Jesus Christ, never by doing what the Law requires. We, too, have believed in Christ Jesus in order to be put right with God through our faith in Christ, and not by doing what the Law requires. For no one is put right with God by doing what the Law requires. Galatians 2:16

For it is by God's grace that you have been saved through faith. It is not the result of your own efforts, but God's gift, so that no one can boast about it. Ephesians 2:8-9

But when the kindness and love of God our Savior was revealed, he saved us. It was not because of any good deeds that we ourselves had done, but because of his own mercy that he saved us. Titus 3:4-5

These verses reveal that:

(1) God has one plan to bring people to Himself and that is through the sacrifice of His Son.
(2) The object of saving faith must be Jesus alone.
(3) Salvation is a gift.
(4) Salvation cannot come through good works.
(5) Salvation cannot come through keeping the Law.
(6) Salvation cannot be bought through gifts to a church.
(7) Confession of sin is made to God—not to man.

We know that a person is put right with God through faith in Christ alone. But how does a person exercise such faith? What must a person do once he knows the way of salvation?

4. Ask Jesus to Save Him

In Romans 10:13, the Bible says, *Everyone who calls out to the Lord for help will be saved.*

Who will call out to the Lord for help? Those who:

(1) Recognize that they are sinners in need of help.

(2) Recognize that Jesus is the Living Son of God, able to forgive all sin and give new life.

(3) Believe fully in Christ alone as Savior and Lord.

(4) Are willing to surrender all of life to the Lordship of Jesus.

To call upon the name of the Lord means to pray, sincerely asking Jesus to forgive your sins and to come into your life as Savior and Lord.

This is how a person is born again.
This is how a person receives eternal life.
This is how a person is saved.
This is how a person is put right with God.

Chapter 7

HOW WILL I RESPOND TO THOSE WHO OPPOSE MY DECISION IF I AM BORN AGAIN?

There is no doubt that others will be influenced if you follow Jesus. Some will be happy for you. Others may be disappointed and unhappy. Unfortunate is the one who does not follow Jesus because of fear of what others will think. Everyone becomes the loser in such a case. This happened in the ministry of Jesus. *Even then, many Jewish authorities believed in Jesus; but because of the Pharisees they did not talk about it openly, so as not to be expelled from the synagogue. They loved the approval of men rather than the approval of God.* John 12:42-43

But some follow and gladly suffer the consequences. What is a person to do when following Jesus causes family members and others to be angry or show disapproval?

First, it is well to remember the words of Jesus Himself when He told about His influence upon society. In Matthew 10:34-37 He says, *Do not think that I have come to bring peace to the world. No, I did not come to bring peace, but a sword. I came to set sons against their fathers, daughters against their mothers, daughters-in-law against their mothers-in-law; a man's worst enemies will be the members of his own family. Whoever loves his father or mother more than me is not fit to be my disciple; whoever loves his sons or daughters more than me is not fit to be my disciple.*

Jesus is saying that conflict will come to families when some members decide to follow Him and the others decide to continue to reject Him. Jesus is not a divider or destroyer of families. The source of the division and strife are those who refuse to follow Christ. The new believer is promoting peace and joy when he receives Christ as his personal Savior and Lord. Though it may appear hopeless for a while, the entire family has a greater chance of being saved because one person dared to be different.

Remember, your goal is the salvation of all your family members and friends, not just the absence of conflict. There are some positive things you can do when you are persecuted for following Jesus.

1. Understand that though other family members are unhappy, you can be happy in your stand for Christ.

Happy are those who are persecuted because they do what God requires; the Kingdom of heaven belongs to them! Happy are you when people insult you and persecute you and tell all kinds of evil lies against you because you are my followers. Be happy and glad, for a great reward is kept for you in heaven.
Matthew 5:10-12

Don't be afraid of your enemies; always be courageous, and this will prove to them that they will lose and that you will win, because it is God who gives you the victory. For you have been given the privilege of serving Christ, not only by believing in him, but also by suffering for him. Philippians 1:28-29

2. Understand that persecution is predicted.

Jesus said, *If they persecuted me, they will persecute you too.*
John 15:20

3. Respond to persecution with love.

The Bible says, *Ask God to bless those who persecute you— yes, ask him to bless, not to curse.* Romans 12:14

4. With patience and persistence pray for the unbelievers in your family.

Jesus said, ...*Love your enemies and pray for those who persecute you.* Matthew 5:44

Paul said, *My brothers, how I wish with all my heart that my own people might be saved! How I pray to God for them!* Romans 10:1

For a time you may be the only member of your family who follows Christ and the Word of God. This can be a difficult time, but always remember the words of the Bible, *Don't worry about anything, but in all your prayers ask God for what you need, always asking him with a thankful heart. And God's peace, which is far beyond human understanding, will keep your hearts and minds safe in union with Christ Jesus...I have the strength to face all conditions by the power that Christ gives me.* Philippians 4:6-7,13

Chapter 8

MAY I CONTINUE TO GO TO MY CHURCH IF I AM BORN AGAIN?

This question is normally asked by those who have not been born again. The answer is: In order to be born again, a person must surrender control of all his life to the Lordship of Jesus Christ. The born again person will gladly follow the Lord of his life—Jesus. All the affairs of life such as education, life's work, choice of a marriage partner, recreation, as well as where and how to worship, will be under the clear direction of our Lord Jesus. Jesus is the one who will determine where a person is to worship. But how do I know what His will is for my life?

We learn God's will for our lives through a daily study of the Bible, His word to His children. Also, the believer will pray daily for God's leadership.

So the question is not, "Can I continue to go to my church?" The question is, "Who will be Lord of my life?" The person who predetermines what he must be able to do is not ready to be born again.

The believer will agree with Paul when he said, *I have been put to death with Christ on his cross, so that it is no longer I who live, but it is Christ who lives in me. This life that I live now, I live by faith in the son of God, who loved me and gave his life for me.* Galatians 2:19-20

Christ, who is Truth (John 14:6), will guide the believer into truth. The true believer will follow what he knows to be truth.

If a person's religion is not based clearly upon the Bible but is based on tradition invented and handed down by men, then the Bible should become that person's new guide.

In Galatians 5:1 Paul was speaking of such a situation when he said, *Freedom is what we have—Christ has set us free! Stand, then, as free people, and do not allow yourselves to become slaves again.*

Concerning people who had been set free (born again), Paul says in Galatians 5:7-8, *You were doing so well! Who made you stop obeying the truth? How did he persuade you? It was not done by God, who calls you.*

Once a person has followed Christ and the way of truth found in the Bible, there may be pressure for him to abandon the truth and go back to his old religion. But as Paul says, this temptation does not come from God and the believer must stay firm and resist the temptation even though there may be threats made against him.

Chapter 9

WHO SHOULD I FOLLOW?

Who we follow will determine where we will spend eternity. Who we follow will determine our quality of life on earth. It is very important, therefore, that we follow the right person.

Who is to receive our highest allegiance? Who will we follow?

If we are to find meaning to life, we must follow the One who has brought meaning to life.

If we are to find victory over death, we must follow the One who has overcome death.

If we are to find victory over sin, we must follow the One who has met and overcome sin.

There is only one person who can claim all of the above victories. It was Jesus. Mohammed sinned, died and stayed in the grave. Buddha sinned, died and stayed in the grave. Joseph Smith sinned, died and stayed in the grave. Mary sinned, died and stayed in the grave. These were good people but they did not have the power to overcome sin and death.

Jesus met life and gave it meaning. He met sin and overcame it. He died and came from the grave to live forever.

Jesus said, *"If anyone wants to come with me, he must forget himself, take up his cross every day, and follow me. For whoever wants to save his own life will lose it, but whoever loses his life for my sake will save it. Will a person gain anything if he wins the whole world but is himself lost or defeated?* Luke 9:23-25

People often prefer to save their lives (their tradition) and in doing so sacrifice their own lives and the lives of all who follow them. This happens when a person says, "I must keep my religion, even if it is different than what the Bible teaches."

Should a child follow his parents?

At a very early age there may not be a choice; small children must follow their parents' desires. But an adult should never follow his parents' religion if it does not follow the truths of God's Word. Children must respect their parents, but must follow Jesus and Him alone. Those children are fortunate whose parents are following Christ and His teachings in the Bible.

Jesus said, *A man's worst enemies will be the members of his own family. Whoever loves his father or mother more than me is not fit to be my disciple; whoever loves his son or daughter more than me is not fit to be my disciple. Whoever does not take up his cross and follow in my steps is not fit to be my disciple.* Matthew 10:36-38

One of the greatest enemies a child has is a parent who is not following Jesus and His teaching. Informed and loving parents will guide their children in Bible study and into a right relationship with God. This right relationship can come only through the new birth. The new birth is possible only through faith in Jesus as the only Savior and Lord.

A person does not lose when he follows Jesus. In Mark 10:28-30 the Bible says, *Then Peter spoke up, "Look, we have left everything and followed you." "Yes," Jesus said to them, "and I tell you that everyone who leaves home or brothers or sisters or mother or father or children or fields for me and for the Gospel, will receive much more in this present age. He will receive a hundred times more houses, brothers, sisters, mothers, children, and fields—and persecutions as well; and in the age to come he will receive eternal life."*

Only those who follow Christ and His teachings will win in this life and in the life to come. A child remaining in the darkness with his parents can offer no help to set his parents free. Only as the child breaks free and follows Biblical teachings can he hope to help his parents know the truth. Rebuke and persecution from parents will be normal because the parents have lost face. They feel that they were already leading their child in the right direction because they know only tradition and not the truth of the Bible.

Should I follow religious leaders?

The religious leaders told Peter to stop preaching about Jesus. We find his response in Acts 4:19-20, *"You yourselves judge which is right in God's sight—to obey you or to obey God. For we cannot stop speaking of what we ourselves have seen and heard."*

Again in Acts 5:29, Peter said to the high priest. *"We must obey God, not men."* Jesus said in Matthew 10:28, *"Do not be afraid of those who kill the body but cannot kill the soul; rather be afraid of God, who can destroy both body and soul in hell."*

When religious leaders warn people about attending Bible studies, who are we to follow? When a religious leader tells you that your children cannot go to school if you study the Bible, who do you follow? The religious leader or Jesus and the Bible?

(We are not speaking about Bible study with cults and groups which are based on human personalities. All must beware of such false religions. We are talking about simple Bible studies with the Bible as the only authority and Jesus as the only head. This is the Christian religion.)

Even though there may be persecution from family, friends, neighbors, and religious leaders, the wise person who is going to heaven must put Jesus first above all and follow Him no matter what others say.

To love Jesus means that we will follow His teachings and do what He tells us to do. In John 14:23-24 Jesus said, *"Whoever loves me will obey my teaching. My Father will love him... Whoever does not love me does not obey my teaching."* Also in John 15:14, Jesus says, *"And you are my friends if you do what I command you."*

Who do I follow?
Jesus Christ is the only one worthy of our total allegiance.

Chapter 10

WHAT ABOUT THE FUNERAL AND BURIAL SERVICES IF I ENTER A NEW RELIGION?

First, as a Bible believer your attitude about death will change. There will no longer be fears of death and returning spirits. Unbelievers usually are ignorant about what the Bible teaches concerning death and eternity.

The Christian (born again believer) will not find it necessary to have bright lights and candles around the casket to keep away spirits. Darkness will no longer be a threat. The fears and superstitions of your former religion will be replaced with hope and security.

While family members will be sad over the death of a loved one, there is hope and joy because of the victory of a certain home in heaven.

The Bible says, *Our brothers, we want you to know the truth about those who have died, so that you will not be sad, as are those who have no hope. We believe that Jesus died and rose again, and so we believe that God will take back with Jesus those who have died believing in him. What we are teaching you now is the Lord's teaching: we who are alive on the day the Lord comes will not go ahead of those who have died. There will be the shout of command, the archangel's voice, the sound of God's trumpet, and the Lord himself will come down from heaven. Those who have died believing in Christ will rise to life first; then we who are living at that time will be gathered up along with them in the clouds to meet the Lord in the air. And so we will always be with the Lord. So then, encourage one another with these words.*
1 Thessalonians 4:13-18

Now that you are informed and know the truth from the **Bible**, you must not be afraid of leaving that religion which has kept you in darkness through its man-made doctrines. Often those doctrines and practices of your old religion have not been designed to bring help and comfort. Rather, as in the case of death and burial, they bring fear and uncertainty.

In your new Biblical religion, what about the funeral and the burial?

When you become a member of a New Testament church, you become a part of a family that loves you and cares about your life, even your death. Your gain is great when you join a church which follows the Bible for its faith and practices.

If a member of your family is sick, there is personal encouragement from the pastor and church members. And if the patient dies, what then? Special counseling and encouragement come from the pastor and church members. In the critical hours before death, the pastor and others will stand by, ready to offer any assistance possible. After the death, depending upon the financial needs of the family, the church often will have a "love offering," which is a voluntary offering to assist the family in meeting their needs related to the funeral expenses.

If needed, the pastor and church members assist in making funeral arrangements.

Church members may take food daily to help the family. On the day of the funeral the church may help provide food for family and friends who come to the home to pay their respects.

The funeral service is planned by the pastor and church members in consultation with family members.

The church provides the place of the service if it has a chapel, and the church will provide the music. The pastor will give a Biblical message. Following the service the pastor will lead the procession from the chapel to the waiting funeral car. The pastor will remain close to the family on the way to the cemetery. At the public cemetery the members of the church often will sing a song of praise and then the pastor will read a passage of hope from the Bible. He then closes the service with prayer. Then many of the church members will offer special words of sympathy and love to the family members.

From the cemetery some of the church members and the pastor will go with the family to their house. There will be a relaxed time of visiting and eating.

Some of the features of your new Christian religion are:

1. People love you. This love is seen in the sacrifices people make to share time, money, and food.

2. There are no mandatory fees from the pastor or the church.

3. The ministry of the pastor is personal. He does not rush through a ceremony and quickly and impersonally walk away and leave you to bury the dead. He gives you his time.

4. Everyone is treated on the same level. The funeral services are the same for the common laborer as for the professional. There are no ordinary and special classes.

5. You now face death with a victorious spirit rather than wailing, gloom and doom.

What about the place for the burial?
(In many underdeveloped nations the following will be helpful.)

These steps should be followed.

1. Obtain a death certificate.
If the person dies in a hospital, the hospital will provide the death certificate.

If the person dies at home, the family physician will prepare a death certificate.

2. Secure a burial permit.
You get this at the treasurer's office at the Municipal Hall. (There is a very small fee.) At the treasurer's office you will be asked where the person will be buried. You will tell them that the burial will be at a public cemetery. (In every town there will be a public cemetery.)

3. Make arrangements for the burial with those in charge of the public cemetery. Normally there is no fee for the burial place. There are some commercial cemeteries where you will have to pay a fee for the burial place.

The place for burial is not a problem for new believers.

In Conclusion:
In sickness and death there is no better place than among believers who love you.

Chapter 11

WHY DO I NEED TO BE BAPTIZED AGAIN?

This question refers to baptism in water and usually comes from a person who does not understand the meaning of Christian baptism. When I say Christian baptism, I am referring to baptism as seen in the Bible.

For most people it is not a question of being baptized again, but of being really baptized the first time. Did you follow the Bible example of baptism? Perhaps a look at what baptism is will help a person know if he has had a Christian baptism.

What is Christian baptism according to the Bible?

There are many examples of baptism in the Scriptures. We will look in detail at one of these.

The story of the Ethiopian official is found in Acts 8:26-39. You may want to read the entire story, but for our purpose, only a portion will be included.

The official asked Philip, "Tell me, of whom is the prophet saying this? Of himself or of someone else?" Then Philip began to speak; starting from this passage of scripture, he told him the Good News about Jesus. As they traveled down the road, they came to a place where there was some water, and the official said, "Here is some water. What is to keep me from being baptized?" Philip said to him, "You may be baptized if you believe with all your heart." "I do," he answered; "I believe that Jesus Christ is the son of God." The official ordered the carriage to stop, and both Philip and the official went down into the water, and Philip baptized him. When they came up out of the water, the

Spirit of the Lord took Philip away. The official did not see him again, but continued on his way, full of joy. Acts 8:34-39

Note some things about this Bible illustration of baptism.

1. The person was an adult when baptized.

2. He heard the Good News about Jesus Christ.

He not only heard, but it is clear that he understood what he was hearing. He was old enough to understand for himself.

3. After he heard the message, he believed that Jesus was the Son of God and the Savior of the World.

This word "believe" is the same one found in other parts of the Bible when the subject is salvation, or eternal life. It meant a complete trust in Christ, and Christ alone, for the forgiveness of sin and the gift of eternal life. Today, born-again Christians are called "believers."

4. This man was baptized **after** he believed.

There are no teachings in the Bible contrary to this order. In the Scriptures, every time a person is baptized, he has already believed in Christ as his Savior and Lord.

5. The official decided personally to believe and to be baptized.

His parents did not decide for him. He was old enough to decide. He did not confer with anyone else about his baptism.

6. The official was immersed in water.

It was not a cup of water; it was a pool of water. Note that the Bible says, ...*both Philip and the official went down into the water, and Philip baptized him. When they came up out of the water...*

Baptism in the Bible was always by immersion. Jesus was immersed. Paul was immersed. All examples of baptism in the Bible were by immersion. The Biblical word *baptize* means immerse.

7. When the official believed and was baptized, he was full of joy. Every person who accepts Christ as his personal Savior and follows the Lord's command to be baptized is full of joy and peace.

If you want to read another example of baptism that is very much like the above story, read Acts 16:29-34.

Note the following verses.

Acts 2:41 - *Peter was preaching and many of them believed his message and were baptized, and about three thousand people were added to the group that day.*

Acts 18:8 - *Crispus, who was the leader of the synagogue, believed in the Lord, together with all his family; and many other people in Corinth heard the message, believed, and were baptized.*

Matthew 28:19-20 - *Go, then, to all peoples everywhere and make them my disciples: baptize them in the name of the Father, the Son and the Holy Spirit, and teach them to obey everything I have commanded you. And I will be with you always, to the end of the age.* This was Christ's command to His disciples.

Acts 19:4-5 - *Paul said, "The baptism of John was for those who turned from their sins; and he told the people of Israel to believe in the one who was coming after him—that is, in Jesus." When they heard this, they were baptized in the name of the Lord Jesus.*

What is Christian baptism?

Bible examples of baptism had the following in common:

1. All were old enough to hear, decide, repent of sin and trust in Christ.

2. All were immersed after they consciously accepted Jesus by faith.

3. All were happy that they had made the decision to believe and to be baptized.

4. All were happy to be related to a "new religion" because they had found the truth and were set free from religious bondage.

Should I be baptized again?

You should be baptized with Christian baptism if you have been born again. You may say, "I don't understand what it means to be born again." If you say this, then you do not qualify for Christian baptism. If you have really been born again, you will have a strong desire to follow the teachings of Jesus concerning baptism. You will not permit others to scare you away from following Bible teachings about baptism or anything else.

If you have not been born again, you have not experienced Christian baptism. It has meaning only for those who have believed. If you have been born again you need to be baptized, not again, but for the first time as far as the Bible is concerned.

God will bless you when you simply follow His Word.

Chapter 12

WHO ARE BAPTISTS?

Baptists are not a religious cult. What is a cult? It is a religion that denies one or more of the basic teachings of the Bible. For example, any religion that denies that Jesus is the Savior is a cult. A religion that denies the Bible as the Word of God is a cult. A religion that accepts tradition and teachings of men to be as authoritative as the Bible is a cult. Usually cults are built upon human personalities, with Christ added. Cults are often based upon the Old Testament. Baptists are not a cult.

The Baptist faith is not a new religion. It is as old as the New Testament. John the Baptist was the first person to be called a Baptist. He prepared people for the coming of Christ. He was called a Baptist because he baptized.

Baptists of today did not choose to be called Baptists. People who persecuted them called them "Anabaptists" because they followed the New Testament example of baptism.

Within the past 200 years Baptists have flourished around the world. Today in the United States, Baptists are one of the strongest religious groups. While there are many different Baptist groups, they share the same basic doctrines.

Who are Baptists?

1. Baptists believe the Bible is the inspired Word of God.

Because it is the inspired Word of God, it is to be believed and used as a guide for living.

Baptists believe Paul's words in 2 Timothy when he said, *All Scripture is inspired by God and is useful for teaching the truth, rebuking error, correcting faults, and giving instruction for right living...* 2 Timothy 3:16

Baptists accept the Bible teaching that no one is to add to or take away from the Scriptures. John says, *Anyone who does not stay with the teaching of Christ, but goes beyond it, does not have God. Whoever does stay with the teaching has both the Father and the Son.* 2 John 1:9

Paul said, *But even if we or an angel from heaven should preach to you a gospel that is different from the one we preached to you, may he be condemned to hell!* Galatians 1:8

2. Baptists believe Jesus Christ is superior to all creation.

The Bible says, *Christ is the visible likeness of the invisible God. He is the first-born Son, superior to all created things. For through him God created everything in heaven and on earth, the seen and the unseen things, including spiritual powers, lords, rulers, and authorities. God created the whole universe through him and for him. Christ existed before all things, and in union with him all things have their proper place. He is the head of his body, the church; he is the source of the body's life. He is the first-born Son, who was raised from death, in order that he alone might have the first place in all things. For it was by God's own decision that the Son has in himself the full nature of God. Through the Son, then, God decided to bring the whole universe back to himself. God made peace through his son's death on the cross and so brought back to himself all things, both on earth and in heaven.* Colossians 1:15-20

From the above Scripture, note some truths which Baptists believe.

(1) Christ is divine.
For it was by God's own decision that the Son has in himself the full nature of God.

(2) Christ is superior.
He is the First-born Son, who was raised from death, in order that he alone might have the first place in all things.
No person or thing is to be put ahead of Christ.

(3) Christ is the head of the church.
He is the head of his body, the church; he is the source of the body's life.

No one can take the place of Christ as head of the church. Baptists have no earthly head or authority. The local church is under the Lordship of Christ. It is not under the authority of an association or convention or any other group. Christ alone is the head.

(4) Christ is the source of salvation.
Through the Son, then, God decided to bring the whole universe back to himself. God made peace through his son's death on the cross and so brought back to himself all things, both on earth and in heaven.

Also we read in Colossians 1:22, *But now, by means of the physical death of his Son, God has made you his friends, in order to bring you, holy, pure, and faultless, into his presence.*

3. Baptists believe that salvation comes only through faith in Christ.

(1) Faith in Christ—not through keeping the Law.

Yet we know that a person is put right with God only through faith in Jesus Christ, never by doing what the Law requires. We, too, have believed in Christ Jesus in order to be put right with

God through our faith in Christ, and not by doing what the Law requires. For no one is put right with God by doing what the Law requires. Galatians 2:16

(2) Faith in Christ—not through doing good works.

For it is by God's grace that you have been saved through faith. It is not the result of your own efforts, but God's gift, so that no one can boast about it. Ephesians 2:8-9

Now that we have been put right with God through faith, we have peace with God through our Lord Jesus Christ. Romans 5:1

(3) Faith in Christ—not rituals (communion, baptism, etc.)

We do not put any trust in external ceremonies. I could, of course, put my trust in such things. If anyone thinks he can trust in external ceremonies, I have even more reason to feel that way. ...As far as a person can be righteous by obeying the commands of the Law, I was without fault. But all those things that I might count as profit I now reckon as loss for Christ's sake. ...For His sake I have thrown everything away; I consider it all as mere garbage, so that I may gain Christ and be completely united with him. I no longer have a righteousness of my own, the kind that is gained by obeying the Law. I now have the righteousness that is given through faith in Christ, the righteousness that comes from God and is based on faith. Philippians 3:3-4, 6-7, 8b-9

4. Baptists believe in the priesthood of every believer.

What does the priesthood of every believer mean? It means two basic things: A **privilege** and a **responsibility**.

Privilege - Every person has access to God through Christ.

But Jesus lives on forever, and his work as priest does not pass on to someone else. And so he is able, now and always, to save those who come to God through him, because he lives forever to plead with God for them. Hebrews 7:24-25

Let us, then, hold firmly to the faith we profess. For we have a great High Priest who has gone into the very presence of God—Jesus, the Son of God. Our High Priest is not one who cannot feel sympathy for our weaknesses. On the contrary, we have a High Priest who was tempted in every way that we are, but did not sin. Let us be brave, then, and approach God's throne, where there is grace. There we will receive mercy and find grace to help us just when we need it. Hebrews 4:14-16

Baptists believe that there is only one High Priest, only one mediator—Jesus. The Bible says, *For there is one God, and there is one who brings God and mankind together, the man Christ Jesus.* 1 Timothy 2:5

Responsibility - Every believer who has received new life through faith in Christ has the responsibility to share that new life with others.

This is clearly seen in 2 Corinthians 5:17-18 where Paul says, *When anyone is joined to Christ, he is a new being; the old is gone, the new has come. All this is done by God, who through Christ changed us from enemies into his friends and gave us the task of making others his friends also.*

Also, we read in 1 Peter 2:9, *But you are a chosen race, the King's priests, the holy nation, God's own people, chosen to proclaim the wonderful acts of God, who called you out of darkness into his own marvelous light.*

This verse tells of the privilege of being God's chosen people. It also tells of the corresponding responsibility to share the Good

News with others. This is what the priesthood of every believer means.

5. Baptists believe that the Good News about Jesus Christ is to be shared with all people.

Baptists accept the mandate of Jesus in Matthew 28:19-20, *Go, then, to all peoples everywhere and make them my disciples: baptize them in the name of the Father, the Son, and the Holy Spirit, and teach them to obey everything I have commanded you. And I will be with you always, to the end of the age.*

6. Baptists believe in religious freedom that allows every person to follow the religion of his choice.

7. Baptists believe in the separation of church and government.

Church officials are not to run the affairs of government, just as government officials are not to run the affairs of the church.

Baptists are free through Christ—free to live a life for Christ, motivated by love—not by fear or duty. Baptists are people of the Book, the Bible. Baptists are people of God, a relationship made possible through faith in His Son, Jesus Christ. Baptists have the responsibility to share Christ with others.

Baptists who have been born again are a peculiar kind of people, people of God. They are victorious and secure in Christ.

Chapter 13

DID MARY CONTINUE TO BE A VIRGIN AFTER THE BIRTH OF JESUS?

The next several questions should be of great interest to both Roman Catholics and Protestants. In pursuing these questions there is no intention of criticizing anyone, but simply to find what the Bible says about these questions.

Before we answer this question, we should learn what the Bible says about Mary. Whatever the Bible teaches should be accepted as God's Word.

According to the Gospels of Matthew and Luke, Mary was a virgin at the time of the birth of Jesus. Beyond the birth of Jesus, the New Testament says very little about her and even the account of Jesus' birth is found in only two of the New Testament books.

There is only one instance during the ministry of Jesus where Mary's words are recorded, and at that time Jesus told her not to tell him what to do. It was at the wedding in Cana, as recorded in John 2:1-5: *Two days later there was a wedding in the town of Cana in Galilee. Jesus' mother was there, and Jesus and his disciples had also been invited to the wedding. When the wine had given out, Jesus' mother said to him, "They are out of wine." "You must not tell me what to do," Jesus replied. "My time has not yet come." Jesus' mother then told the servants, "Do whatever he tells you."*

This was at the very beginning of the ministry of Jesus. Mary appears only twice throughout the record of the rest of His earthly ministry. Once when Jesus was speaking to the multitudes, Mary and the brothers of Jesus came looking for Him. Jesus rebuked them by saying, "*Who is my mother? Who are my brothers?*" (Matthew 12:46ff) The other time was when He was on the cross and asked His especially loved disciple, John, to care for His mother. (John 19:25-27)

The last time Mary is mentioned in the Bible is in Acts 1:14. This was shortly after the death and resurrection of Jesus. Speaking of the disciples the verse says: *They gathered frequently to pray as a group, together with the women and with Mary the mother of Jesus and with his brothers.* She is not given a place of prominence or even special recognition.

According to the Bible, the apostles never prayed to Mary or gave her a special place of honor. Peter, James, and John never mention her name in the letters they wrote to the churches. John took care of her until she died but he never mentioned her name in the four books of the Bible which he wrote. Paul wrote more than half of the entire New Testament and he never once mentioned Mary.

When the New Testament Church was started there was only one name declared to be Savior and that was Jesus: *Salvation is to be found through him alone; in all the world there is no one else whom God has given who can save us.* Acts 4:12

To find the attitude of Jesus toward his mother read John 2:1-5 and Matthew 12:46-50.

Now to the question, **"Did Mary continue to be a virgin after the birth of Jesus?"**

The Bible teaches that Mary was a virgin when Jesus was born. But what about after the birth of Jesus? Did Mary become Joseph's wife? Did Joseph and Mary have other children?

From the Bible we read: *So when Joseph woke up, he married Mary, as the angel of the Lord had told him to. But he had no sexual relations with her before she gave birth to her son. And Joseph named him Jesus.* Matthew 1:24-25

The emphasis is that he did not have sexual relations with Mary before the birth of Christ.

To man and woman, husband and wife, God said at the beginning of creation, "Go forth and multiply." For Joseph and Mary to act as married partners and thus have children is simply following God's will. It was normal. It was not degrading for Mary to fulfill her responsibilities as a loving wife and mother.

The Scripture speaks of Jesus as the first born of Mary which clearly indicates there were others who followed. How many children did Joseph and Mary have after she gave birth to Jesus? The Bible tells us the names of some of them. In Matthew 13:53-55 we read: *When Jesus finished telling these parables, he left that place and went back to his home town. He taught in the synagogue, and those who heard him were amazed. "Where did he get such wisdom?" they asked. "And what about his miracles? Isn't he the carpenter's son? Isn't Mary his mother, and aren't James, Joseph, Simon and Judas his brothers? Aren't all his sisters living here?"*

In Mark 6:3, we read: *"Isn't he the carpenter, the son of Mary, and the brother of James, Joseph, Judas, and Simon? Aren't his sisters living here?"*

In John 7:5 we read: *Not even his brothers believed in him.*

In Psalm 69:8 we read a prophecy about the coming Christ.
I am like a stranger to my brother, like a foreigner to my family.

A serious student of the Bible will not deny that Joseph and Mary were really husband and wife and that they had other children.

What then are we to think about Mary?

We are to believe all that the Holy Scripture teaches—nothing more and nothing less. Mary was a virtuous, good, humble, and committed woman. She is to be honored because God chose her to be the mother of the Savior. But she is not to be prayed to, worshipped, or made to be central in the Christian religion. To do so is to go beyond and contrary to the teachings of the Scripture.

Some say they reach God through praying to Mary because she has a tender and understanding heart. What does the Bible say?

For there is one God, and there is one who brings God and mankind together, the man Christ Jesus, who gave himself to redeem all mankind. 1 Timothy 2:5-6

Let us, then, hold firmly to the faith we profess. For we have a great High Priest who has gone into the very presence of God—Jesus, the Son of God. Our High Priest is not one who cannot feel sympathy for our weaknesses. On the contrary, we have a High Priest who was tempted in every way that we are, but did not sin. Let us be brave, then, and approach God's throne, where there is grace. There we will receive mercy and find grace to help us just when we need it. Hebrews 4:14-16

A true Christian will not:	pray to Mary.
	bow to Mary.
	expect help from Mary.
	retain images of Mary.

Chapter 14

WHAT IS CHRISTIAN PRAYER?

Prayer is a great privilege of the believer. We will answer four questions concerning prayer.

1. What is prayer?
2. Why should I pray?
3. How do I pray?
4. When do I pray?

WHAT IS PRAYER?

Through the Bible, God talks to man. Through prayer, man talks to God. Prayer is communication with God. Prayer is spending time with God, talking to him and listening for his answer.

In Matthew 6:9, Jesus said, *This, then is how you should pray: Our Father in Heaven...*

In Matthew 6:6, *But when you pray, go to your room, close the door, and pray to your Father, who is unseen. And your Father, who sees what you do in private, will reward you.*

These verses show that prayer is talking to God. Prayer is not talking to man.

When we were born again, God became our Father and we became his children. In John 1:12-13 we read, *Some, however, did receive him and believed in him; so he gave them the right to become God's children. They did not become God's children by natural means, that is, by being born as children of a human father; God himself was their Father.*

From these verses we find the basis for prayer. That basis is a Father-child relationship brought about by the new birth. Prayer is the privilege of the believer because of his new relationship with God as his Father. Prayer is a natural relationship of a father and child. Because God is our Father, we share with him our dreams, goals, problems, and praise. This is prayer.

WHY SHOULD I PRAY?

It is the natural thing to do. Our special relationship to God matures when we pray. God is our best and most trusted friend; therefore, we need to talk to him.

How do I thank God for daily blessings? Through prayer. The Bible says, *Be joyful always, pray at all times, be thankful in all circumstances. This is what God wants from you in your life in union with Christ Jesus.* 1 Thessalonians 5:16-18

How do I receive forgiveness of sins? Through prayer. The Bible says, *But if we confess our sins to God, he will keep his promise and do what is right; he will forgive us our sins and purify us from all wrongdoing.* 1 John 1:9 A good example of prayer for forgiveness is found in Psalm 51.

How do I make my needs known to God? Through prayer. The Bible says, *Let us be brave, then, and approach God's throne, where there is grace. There we will receive mercy and find grace to help us just when we need it.* Hebrews 4:16

But if any of you lacks wisdom, he should pray to God, who will give it to him; because God gives generously and graciously to all. James 1:5

Why should I pray?
- ◆ Because it is natural for a child to talk to his Father.
- ◆ Because I need to express my thankfulness to God.

- ◆ Because I need forgiveness of sins.
- ◆ Because I need to make my needs known to God.
- ◆ Christ felt the need to pray. So must we.

HOW SHOULD I PRAY?

The disciples of Jesus said, *Lord, teach us to pray.* (Luke 11:1) Before Jesus taught his disciples how to pray, he warned them against wrong ways to pray. He said, *"When you pray, do not be like the hypocrites! They love to stand up and pray in the houses of worship and on the street corners, so that everyone will see them. I assure you, they have already been paid in full. When you pray, do not use a lot of meaningless words, as the pagans do, who think that God will hear them because their prayers are long."* Matthew 6:5,7

Jesus continued speaking to his disciples about prayer. *"This, then, is how you should pray: 'Our Father in heaven: May your holy name be honored; may your Kingdom come; may your will be done on earth as it is in heaven. Give us today the food we need. Forgive us the wrongs we have done, as we forgive the wrongs that others have done to us. Do not bring us to hard testings, but keep us safe from the Evil One.* Matthew 6:9-13

This is called the model prayer. Jesus did not mean that believers should always repeat these exact words. When we read the prayers of Jesus and Paul in the New Testament, we see that they do not repeat these words. Jesus is saying that prayer includes: praise and honor to God, obedience to the will of God, seeking God's help for daily needs such as food, confession of sin, and request for help in overcoming Satan, the Evil One. In our prayers we should be concerned about the same things found in the Model Prayer.

As a new believer, how should I learn to pray?

1. When you are alone, speak aloud to God.
2. You are not making a speech to God. Simply express your thoughts to him.
3. Remember your prayers are from your heart to God.
4. Pray with a family member or friend.
5. Pray every time before you eat, thanking God for his provisions.

WHEN DO I PRAY?

The new Christian should pray his first prayer immediately after he has been born again. That prayer may be something like this, "Jesus, thank you for saving me."

A grateful Christian will pray **before every meal**, expressing thanks. It is best to **begin the day** with prayer, seeking God's guidance and protection throughout the day. At the **end of the day** or before sleeping, pray, thanking God for his guidance and protection throughout the day and for all other blessings.

This would establish a pattern of **five regular times** every day when some special time is given to prayer. The believer will find it natural to pray spontaneously throughout the day. You can pray as you walk, ride, etc.

A Christian must read the Bible and pray regularly if he is to be healthy spiritually. You may want to read some other verses about prayer.

Daniel 6:10   Matthew 18:20   Matthew 26:41   Luke 18:1
1 Thessalonians 5:17   Matthew 7:7   Mark 11:25   John 17

Chapter 15

SHOULD I USE THE ROSARY IN PRAYER?

It may help if we look at the origin and the use of the rosary before answering this question.

Peter the Hermit invented the rosary in the year 1090, more than a thousand years after the death of Christ. Its use did not become common until the 13th century. It was not officially sanctioned until after the Protestant reformation in the sixteenth century.

A mechanical device was used in counting prayers by the Buddhists and the Mohammedans for centuries before the introduction of the rosary.

What is the rosary?

1. It is a series of prayers. In its long form it has 15 Pater-nosters (The Lord's Prayer, addressed to God the Father), 15 Glorias, and 150 Hail Marys addressed to the "virgin Mary."

2. It is a mechanical devise used in counting prayers. The shorter and more common form is a string of beads divided into five sections, each consisting of one large bead and ten small beads. The large rosary has fifteen sections. Normally, when a person wants to say the complete rosary, he will go over the short form three times.

The word "rosary" means, a garland of roses. There is a legend that says that "Our Lady" was seen to take rosebuds from the lips of a young monk when he was reciting Hail Marys, and she wove them into a garland which he placed on her head.

The rosary has ten times as many prayers addressed to Mary as to God. In the rosary no prayers are addressed to Jesus or the Holy Spirit. A human being is exalted above God or Jesus Christ in the use of the rosary.

What does the Bible teach about using such forms of prayer as represented by the rosary?

Jesus said, *When you pray, do not use a lot of meaningless words, as the pagans do, who think that God will hear them because their prayers are long. Do not be like them...This, then, is how you should pray: 'Our Father in heaven: May your holy name be honored; May your kingdom come; may your will be done on earth as it is in heaven. Give us today the food we need. Forgive us the wrongs we have done, as we forgive the wrongs that others have done to us.'* Matthew 6:7-12

From this clear teaching of Jesus we learn:

1. God is to be addressed when we pray. Jesus said, "Our Father."

2. No mechanical device was suggested.

3. Jesus prayed often, and He always prayed spontaneously from His heart. He always prayed to His Father. He never mentioned Mary in His prayers and He did not advise anyone else to do so.

Some people say they pray to Mary because she is motherly and understands our sin and will appeal to God on our behalf. See what the Bible has to say.

Let us, then, hold firmly to the faith we profess. For we have a great High Priest who has gone into the very presence of God—Jesus, the Son of God. Our High Priest is not one who cannot feel sympathy for our weaknesses. On the contrary, we have a

High Priest who was tempted in every way that we are, but did not sin. Let us be brave, then, and approach God's throne, where there is grace. There we will receive mercy and find grace to help us just when we need it. Hebrews 4:14-16

In 1 Timothy 2:5 we read: *For there is one God, and there is one who brings God and mankind together, the man Christ Jesus.*

A person does not need to be a religious leader or a scholar to understand what these verses are teaching. A person need not go through another person or a mechanical device to get to God. Jesus is the only possible way to reach God in prayer and receive forgiveness of sin. The Bible says that Jesus feels sympathy for our weaknesses. Read the verses from Hebrews again. It is God's Word and is true.

The conclusion is: The rosary was not used by Jesus, Peter, Paul or anyone else in the Bible. Therefore why should we use it today? A Christian will not use the rosary after he learns what the Bible teaches.

Prayer is important. Prayer is a beautiful communion between God and His children. As a follower of the Bible, the Christian should follow the Bible teachings about prayer.

Chapter 16

WHAT DOES THE BIBLE TEACH ABOUT IMAGES OR IDOLS?

The Ten Commandments are fundamental laws which God gave to His people. These are found in Exodus 20. The first five verses say, *God spoke, and these were His words: "I am the Lord your God who brought you out of Egypt, where you were slaves. Worship no god but me. Do not make for yourselves images of anything in heaven or on earth or in the water under the earth. Do not bow down to any idol or worship it, because I am the Lord your God and I tolerate no rivals."*

Again the Bible says, *For your own good, then, make certain that you do not sin by making for yourselves an idol in any form at all —whether man or woman, animal or bird, reptile or fish.* Deuteronomy 4:15-18

The Lord said, "Do not make idols or set up statues, stone pillars, or carved stones to worship." Leviticus 26:1

What does the Bible say about idols or images in the home?

From Deuteronomy 7:26 we read: *Do not bring any of these idols into your homes, or the same curse will be on you that is on them. You must hate and despise these idols, because they are under the Lord's curse.*

In the New Testament Paul says, *...the news about your faith in God has gone everywhere. There is nothing, then, that we need to say. All those people speak about how you received us when we visited you, and how you turned away from idols to God, to serve the true and living God.* 1 Thessalonians 1:8-9

In 1 Corinthians 12:1-2 Paul says, *I want you to know the truth about them, my brothers. You know that while you were still heathen, you were led astray in many ways to the worship of lifeless idols.*

From the books of Isaiah and Jeremiah in the Old Testament we find more than sixty references to idols, images, or statues. On every occasion there is a strong condemnation for anyone who has anything to do with them. If you want to know why life is so difficult today, please read these two books and you will see that God promises punishment and curses on anyone who makes, honors, bows down to, or has anything to do with images or statutes. Notice the following verses.

A time is coming when all of you will throw away the sinful idols you made out of silver and gold. Isaiah 31:7 *I will not let idols share my praise.* Isaiah 42:8

All those who make idols are worthless, and the gods they prize so highly are useless. Isaiah 44:9

With some of the wood he makes a fire; he roasts meat, eats it, and is satisfied. He warms himself and says, "How nice and warm! What a beautiful fire!" The rest of the wood he makes into an idol, and then he bows down and worships it. He prays to it and says, "You are my god—save me!" Such people are too stupid to know what they are doing. They close their eyes and their minds to the truth. Isaiah 44:16-18

They have placed their idols, which I hate, in my Temple and have defiled it. Jeremiah 7:30

Such idols are like scarecrows in a field of melons. Jeremiah 10:5 *I will make them pay double for their sin and wickedness, because they have defiled my land with idols that are as lifeless as corpses.* Jeremiah 16:18

What does the Bible say about religious leaders who lead people to use idols and images in worship or in the home?

God's anger is revealed from heaven against all the sin and evil of the people whose evil ways prevent the truth from being known. God punishes them, because what can be known about God is plain to them, for God himself made it plain. Ever since God created the world, his invisible qualities, both his eternal power and his divine nature, have been clearly seen; they are perceived in the things that God has made. So those people have no excuse at all! They know God, but they do not give him the honor that belongs to him, nor do they thank him. Instead, their thoughts have become complete nonsense, and their empty minds are filled with darkness. They say they are wise, but they are fools; instead of worshipping the immortal God, they worship images made to look like mortal man or birds or animals or reptiles. And so God has given those people over to do the filthy things their hearts desire, and they do shameful things with each other. They exchange the truth about God for a lie. Romans 1:18-25

From these verses you can form your own opinion about the use of images or statues in the place of worship or in the home.

In all the Bible you will never find a positive statement about using statues or images in worship. Always it is condemned.

What is the believer to do with the statues and images left from his old religion? Pray to God and ask Him what you should do. He will lead you.

The Christian will want to be obedient to Biblical teachings.

Chapter 17

WHAT DOES THE BIBLE TEACH ABOUT PURGATORY AND PRAYING FOR THE DEAD?

There is no place in the Bible that teaches that prayer should be offered for the dead. No passage of Scripture implies that this should be done. Jesus never mentioned prayer for the dead. The apostles never mentioned it. The custom seems to have come into practice at the end of the second century. The church of Rome took advantage of this practice relating it to the non-Biblical doctrine of purgatory in a scheme to make money from the rich and the poor alike. What does the Bible say about this?

Concerning death, Paul said, *I am pulled in two directions. I want very much to leave this life and be with Christ, which is a far better thing...* Philippians 1:23

In 2 Corinthians 5:6,8, Paul said, *So we are always full of courage. We know that as long as we are at home in the body we are away from the Lord's home. We are full of courage and would much prefer to leave our home in the body and be at home with the Lord.*

When Jesus died on the cross, one of the thieves who died with him repented of his sin and asked Jesus to remember him. The Bible says, *And he said to Jesus, "Remember me, Jesus, when you come as King!" Jesus said to him, "I promise you that today you will be in Paradise with me."* Luke 23:42-43

In Luke 16:19-31 Jesus told a story about the state of man following death.

"There was once a rich man who dressed in the most expensive clothes and lived in great luxury every day. There was also a poor man named Lazarus, covered with sores, who used to be brought to the rich man's door, hoping to eat the bits of food that fell from the rich man's table. Even the dogs would come and lick his sores. The poor man died and was carried by the angels to sit beside Abraham at the feast in heaven. The rich man died and was buried, and in Hades, where he was in great pain, he looked up and saw Abraham, far away, with Lazarus at his side. So he called out, 'Father Abraham! Take pity on me, and send Lazarus to dip his finger in some water and cool off my tongue, because I am in great pain in this fire!' But Abraham said, 'Remember, my son, that in your lifetime you were given all the good things, while Lazarus got all the bad things. But now he is enjoying himself here, while you are in pain. Besides all that, there is a deep pit lying between us, so that those who want to cross over from here to you cannot do so, nor can anyone cross over to us from where you are.' The rich man said, 'Then I beg you, father Abraham, send Lazarus to my father's house, where I have five brothers. Let him go and warn them so that they, at least, will not come to this place of pain.' Abraham said, 'Your brothers have Moses and the prophets to warn them; your brothers should listen to what they say.' The rich man answered, 'That is not enough, father Abraham! But if someone were to rise from death and go to them, then they would turn from their sins.' But Abraham said, 'If they will not listen to Moses and the prophets, they will not be convinced even if someone were to rise from death.'"

Jesus said, "I am the Light of the world, whoever follows me will have the light of life and will never walk in darkness." John 8:12

This is the hope of all who have been born again. Based on the promise of Jesus, they will **never** walk in darkness. There is no purgatory for them.

Concerning the future home of those who have not been born again, Paul said, *I have told you this many times before, and now I repeat it with tears: there are many whose lives make them enemies of Christ's death on the cross. They are going to end up in hell...* Philippians 3:18-19

In the Sermon on the Mount Jesus spoke of the future home of those who are born again and those who are not. *"Go in through the narrow gate, because the gate to hell is wide and the road that leads to it is easy, and there are many who travel it. But the gate to life is narrow and the way that leads to it is hard, and there are few people who find it."* Matthew 7:13-14

Conclusions based on the Word of God are:

1. There are two destinations: heaven and hell.

2. The time of deciding where a person will spend eternity is in this life. The story of the rich man and Lazarus tells us that after death the time of decision is past.

3. The stories of the rich man and Lazarus and the thief on the cross reveals that immediately following death, a person goes to hell or to heaven.

4. The story of the rich man and Lazarus also reveals the painful truth that once a person is dead and goes to hell, there is no hope of salvation, therefore prayer for that person is useless. Prayer for the dead is a false hope.

5. Since purgatory is not mentioned in the Bible, there is no need to pray for a person's soul to be transferred from purgatory.

6. The doctrine of prayer for the dead and its companion doctrine of purgatory are contrary to Bible teachings.

7. It may not be dangerous to put off some things, but when it comes to making a decision to follow Christ and His teachings, it is very dangerous to think, "Someday when I have time..." God's mercy goes up to the last breath of man, but not beyond.

Chapter 18

DO I NEED TO FEAR EVIL SPIRITS AFTER I AM BORN AGAIN?

The native religion of many underdeveloped nations is animism. This is a religion based on superstition and fear and is found in varying degrees around the world. I first became aware of animism when I was a missionary in the Philippines.

When the Spanish conquered the Philippines, they brought with them Catholicism. The Philippines accepted Catholicism, but incorporated with it their native animism. Even though the Philippines is known as a Christian nation, animism is still very much a part of the Philippine culture. The presence of statues in homes, businesses, and in automobiles reveals an animistic nature.

What is animism? Some define it as spirit worship. It is the belief that everything is controlled by spirits. The spirits may attach themselves to objects, such as trees, a mountain, or a river. It is a belief that physical objects possess a spirit of their own. These spirits reveal themselves at different times through objects, people, or places. They may be spirits only, or they may be spirits of the dead. The spirits usually are feared and sometimes are worshipped. Often certain people, such as the witch doctors and mediums, can contact and control the spirits.

Note some examples of animism as I saw it in the Philippines.

Multo - the spirit of a dead person returning as a giant.

Asuwant - the spirit of a dead person who turns himself into an animal, such as a dog. This dog roams around at night seeking victims. Some people burn rubber at dusk so that the bad smell will keep away the evil spirit.

Albularyo - This is the medicine man. He may use "black magic" to bring a curse upon someone.

Fetishism-amulets - Some use the anting-anting. It is a small pouch made of old cloth and contains small pieces of buttons, string, hair, etc. Children wear it around their necks or pin it to their clothing. This is to protect them from harm or sickness.

Magic charms - These are common. They are supposed to protect a person from harm.

Worship of Idols and Images - There is saint San Jose for carpenters, Our Lady of Perpetual Help for the sick, Our Lady of Fatima for debtors, etc.

Animism is a religion of fear and superstition. It offers no mercy or love. There is an absence of hope and peace. Animism is similar to spiritualism. Spiritualism is the belief that the living can communicate with the spirits of the dead. Spiritualists have meetings called seances. There is a time of meditation, after which a person known as a "medium" will go into a trance. The body of the medium will be taken over by a spirit. This spirit is supposedly the spirit of someone who has died. The spirit will talk to the medium or through the medium to the group. Sometimes things of the past, present, or the future will be revealed.

What does the Bible say about animism and spiritualism?

First, it **does not deny** the existence of evil and supernatural spirits.

The Bible is full of warnings concerning trying to talk with the dead, the use of magic, idols, and statues. There are warnings against going to astrologers and fortunetellers. There are warnings against supernatural spirits which are not of God. We will note some of these verses from the Bible.

Concerning consulting mediums, the Bible says, *But people will tell you to ask for messages from fortunetellers and mediums, who chirp and mutter. They will say, "After all, people should ask for messages from the spirits and consult the dead on behalf of the living." You are to answer them, "Listen to what the Lord is teaching you! Don't listen to mediums—what they tell you will do you no good."* Isaiah 8:19-20

God's Word is very clear on this matter. The believer should never try to talk with the spirits of the dead.

Concerning fortunetellers and astrologers, God said, *"I make fools of fortunetellers and frustrate the predictions of astrologers."* Isaiah 44:25

Concerning evil spirits, the Bible says, *One day as we were going to the place of prayer, we were met by a slave girl who had an evil spirit that enabled her to predict the future. She earned a lot of money for her owners by telling fortunes. She followed Paul and us, shouting, "These men are servants of the Most High God! They announce to you how you can be saved!" She did this for many days, until Paul became so upset that he turned around and said to the spirit, "In the name of Jesus Christ I order you to come out of her!" The spirit went out of her that very moment.* Acts 16:16-18

This young girl had a powerful evil spirit. Paul recognized that it was not a spirit from God, therefore it was undesirable and dangerous.

Concerning those who do miracles, the Bible says, *"Then if anyone says to you, 'Look, here is the Messiah!' or 'There he is!'*

— do not believe him. For false Messiahs and false prophets will appear; they will perform great miracles and wonders in order to deceive even God's chosen people, if possible. Listen! I have told you this ahead of time." Matthew 24:23-25

A prophet or an interpreter of dreams may promise a miracle or a wonder, in order to lead you to worship and serve gods that you have not worshipped before. Even if what he promises comes true, do not pay any attention to him. The Lord your God is using him to test you, to see if you love the Lord with all your heart. Follow the Lord and have reverence for him; obey him and keep his commands; worship him and be faithful to him. Deuteronomy 13:1-4

The Wicked One will come with the power of Satan and perform all kinds of false miracles and wonders, and use every kind of wicked deceit on those who will perish. 2 Thessalonians 2:9-10a

The believer has victory over Satan and evil spirits. The believer has a new power in his life when he accepts Christ. The Holy Spirit comes to live in him. The believer does not need to seek further for supernatural spirits, because the true Spirit of God lives in his life to control and protect. There are evil spirits in the world, but they have no power to hurt the believer. As the believer reads the Bible he learns that God revealed Himself through His son, Jesus. God continues to reveal Himself through the Holy Scripture. God does not live in objects such as trees or rocks, but He lives in the lives of His people—those who have been born again.

The key to the believer's victory over demons and evil spirits is seen in Ephesians 6:10-13. *Finally, build up your strength in union with the Lord and by means of his mighty power. Put on all the armor that God gives you, so that you will be able to stand up against the Devil's evil tricks. For we are not fighting against human beings but against the wicked spiritual forces in the heavenly world, the rulers, authorities, and cosmic powers of this dark age. So put on God's armor now! Then when the evil day comes, you will be able to resist the enemy's attacks; and after fighting to the end, you will still hold your ground.* (Read Ephesians 6:14-18 for more details about the armor.)

A story in the Bible shows us that evil spirits are real, yet subject to the power of Jesus Christ. In Luke 8:26-33 we read: *Jesus and his disciples sailed on over to the territory of Gerasa, which is across the lake from Galilee. As Jesus stepped ashore, he was met by a man from the town who had demons in him. For a long time this man had gone without clothes and would not stay at home, but spent his time in the burial caves. When he saw Jesus, he gave a loud cry, threw himself down at his feet, and shouted, "Jesus, Son of the Most High God! What do you want with me? I beg you, don't punish me!" He said this because Jesus had ordered the evil spirit to go out of him. Many times it had seized him, and even though he was kept a prisoner, his hands and feet tied with chains, he would break the chains and be driven by the demon out into the desert. Jesus asked him, "What is your name?" "My name is 'Mob,'" he answered—because many demons had gone into him. The demons begged Jesus not to send them into the abyss. There was a large herd of pigs near by, feeding on a hillside. So the demons begged Jesus to let them go into the pigs, and he let them. They went out of the man and into the pigs. The whole herd rushed down the side of the cliff into the lake and was drowned.*

Evil spirits existed and had power over a man, but Christ had complete authority over the evil spirits. Every believer can claim this authority over all powers of evil. *The seventy-two men came back in great joy. "Lord," they said, "even the demons obeyed us when we gave them a command in your name!"* Luke 10:17

Conclusion
God has power to and does perform miracles. But Satan can also perform miracles. He can use things and people in supernatural ways to deceive people. He can use magic, charms, fetishes, amulets, quack doctors, mediums, astrologers and fortune-tellers. Satan can even use people who are very religious, who use the name of Christ in all they do. People can perform miracles of healing, yet not be from God. (Read Matthew 7:21-23) Because there are evil spirits disguised in what appears to be good, the believer must be very careful. Many people will believe that everything of miraculous nature is from God. This is dangerous because Satan will lead such people astray and to their physical and spiritual death. The Bible says, *My dear friends, do not believe all who claim to have the Spirit, but test them to find out if the spirit they have comes from God. For many false prophets have gone out everywhere.* 1 John 4:1

The Apostle Paul said, *All those people speak about how you received us when we visited you, and how you turned from idols to God, to serve the true and living God and to wait for his Son to come from heaven—His Son Jesus, whom he raised from death and who rescues us from God's anger that is coming.* 1 Thessalonians 1:9-10

We see several things in these verses:

1. They speak of believers turning from such things as idols, charms, or any other thing thought to contain supernatural power.

2. They speak of the only worthy object of faith and allegiance. That object of faith is the true and living God as seen in the Bible and revealed through His Son, Jesus.

3. They speak of a hope in the life of the believer for the coming again of Jesus.

4. They speak of the only source of security—Jesus, the One who overcame death and "rescues" us, or saves us.

Additional Scripture to read:
The dead cannot come back to speak -   Luke 16:19-31
Consulting the spirit of the dead. -   Leviticus 19:31
                                        1 Chronicles 10:13
                                        2 Kings 21:6

Chapter 19

SHOULD I HAVE MY BABY BAPTIZED?

There is not one example of a baby baptism in all the Bible. There is not one word in the Bible about baby baptism.

Why, then, do so many people have their babies baptized? This is nothing more than a tradition. It has no Bible basis. People who have their babies baptized are blindly following those leaders who are also blind spiritually. Those who know the Bible will never consider having their babies baptized.

What does the Bible teach about baptism?

Jesus was about 30 years old when He was baptized.

The Bible says that after Peter had finished his message, *Many of them believed his message and were baptized.* Acts 2:41

Peter said, *"These people have received the Holy Spirit, just as we also did. Can anyone, then, stop them from being baptized with water?"* Acts 10:47

Paul's baptism is recorded in the 9th chapter of Acts. Paul was at least middle aged at this time.

Acts 8 tells of the baptism of an Ethiopian government official. He first heard the Good News and believed, then he was baptized.

Acts 16 tells of a Philippian jail guard who believed and then was baptized.

None of these were babies.

They all believed in Jesus Christ as the only way to heaven. After they believed, they chose to be baptized.

Baptism before one has chosen to trust Christ is totally meaningless. Biblical baptism must follow the New Birth.

But what will happen to a baby if he dies without being baptized?

A child is innocent until he is old enough to hear the Gospel, understand that he is a sinner, repent of that sinful condition, and personally trust in Christ as Savior and Lord. The Bible says that those who will receive God's punishment are those who hear the Gospel and refuse to accept Christ as Savior and Lord. John 3:18 says, *Whoever believes in the Son is not judged; but whoever does not believe has already been judged, because he has not believed in God's only Son.*

Is a person judged or condemned because he has not been baptized? No, he is condemned because he does not believe in Christ as his own personal Lord.

A baby cannot make a decision to place faith in Christ. He cannot repent of sin.

But what will happen if my baby dies?

In the Bible we find a clear answer:

David prayed to God that the child would get well. He refused to eat anything, and every night he went into his room and spent the night lying on the floor. His court officials went to him and tried to make him get up, but he refused and would not eat anything with them. A week later the child died, and David's officials were afraid to tell him the news. They said, "While the child was living,

David wouldn't answer us when we spoke to him. How can we tell him that his child is dead? He might do himself some harm!" When David noticed them whispering to each other, he realized that the child had died. So he asked them, "Is the child dead?" "Yes, he is," they answered. David got up from the floor, took a bath, combed his hair, and changed his clothes. Then he went and worshipped in the house of the Lord. When he returned to the palace, he asked for food and ate it as soon as it was served. "We don't understand this," his officials said to him. "While the child was alive, you wept for him and would not eat; but as soon as he died, you got up and ate!" "Yes," David answered, "I did fast and weep while he was still alive. I thought that the Lord might be merciful to me and not let the child die. But now that he is dead, why should I fast? Could I bring the child back to life? I will some day go to where he is, but he can never come back to me."
2 Samuel 12:16-23

What do we learn from this Scripture?

1. David realized that the baby had gone to heaven and he would one day see the baby again in heaven.

2. The baby did not have any special last rites or baptism. It is well that we remember that God said concerning David, "He is a man after my own heart." David was a great man of God. He trusted God to take care of his baby. His baby was innocent of rebellion and unbelief.

A Christian who follows the Bible will not be concerned about having his baby baptized. Parents should be concerned about raising their children to know the Bible so that one day they can trust in Christ. This is the responsibility of parents.

You may say, "How can we name our child without baby baptism?"

You can do it the same way millions of other believers do it. Many do not baptize babies, yet they give their babies names.

But, can they go to school without a baptismal certificate? Yes, without any question. Schools are filled with children from homes where baby baptism is not practiced. A birth certificate is all that is needed to prove the age of a child.

What about a dedication service?

Many Christian churches have dedication services for newborn babies. This does not make the baby a Christian nor bring him salvation.

A dedication service is a time when the parents publicly commit themselves to bring up the child in such a way that he will come to love the Bible, and to accept the Lord Jesus as his personal Savior. Often the dedication service is held as a part of the regular worship service of the church. The church may give a dedication certificate to the parents.

Conclusion

The Bible is the believer's guide. Therefore believers should not baptize babies.

Chapter 20

WHAT ABOUT THE SALVATION OF CHILDREN?

1. Children are important - Matthew 18:1-7

2. It is important that children be taught.

    (1) What is taught is important.

    (2) Who teaches is important.
    - A. The teacher should be an active, proven member of the local church.
    - B. The teacher should be well-founded in basic Bible doctrines.
    - C. The teacher should be approved by the church before being allowed to teach.
    - D. The teacher should be trained by the local church in techniques of teaching children.

3. Primary sources of children's education.

    (1) Christian ideal
    - A. Home
    - B. Church
    - C. School

    (2) Today's norm
    - A. Mass media—radio, television, movies, print
    - B. School/peers
    - C. Home
    - D. Church

4. Children and the church

   (1) The church provides children opportunities to:
      A. Develop in Bible knowledge
      B. Participate in and learn to appreciate worship
      C. Develop Christian social interaction.

   (2) The children of the church will be the church of tomorrow.

A regenerate (born again) church membership is basic to the life and health of the church. Therefore, it is of utmost importance that boys and girls, who are to be the church of tomorrow, have a genuine conversion experience. A shallow and partial view of salvation urged upon children will result in a weakened or dead church of tomorrow.

The church must take seriously its responsibility to children. A child saved and unrelated to a church family will find it almost impossible to develop spiritually. Practically, what does this mean?

A child born in the flesh should be related to a family. A child born again should be related to a church family.

Some may be so concerned that children be saved that they fail to think of the nurture and development of the child in the church.

This means that when I think of the spiritual birth of a child, I should have foresight to think about how the child will be fed spiritually.

It was no mistake when Jesus called adults to form the early church to be an agent of world evangelism. The evangelization of children is the fruit of the church. The church has a responsibility to teach, educate, evangelize, and finally, to nurture the children.

Adequate time must be given in the teaching/education process before a child is ready to be saved. Teachers of children must have a clear understanding of the Biblical view of salvation.

A teacher with a shallow view of salvation will expect very young children to quickly accept that same view and be ready for salvation after a few short lessons.

The primary task of the Sunday School teacher is to saturate the minds of children with the Word of God. This will include telling Bible stories, sharing direct Bible teachings, and memorizing Scripture.

Because children are so eager to please an adult, the teacher must be very careful about giving "invitations." Even among children, the Holy Spirit must be the one to convince, convict, and call. Many children easily say "yes" to certain questions and then are assured by the teacher that they are saved when the children have never felt a conviction and urging by the Holy Spirit.

A child who is led to make a false decision is in a worse condition than he was before the decision. After posing as a Christian for years, it is very difficult for a person to admit that he made a mistake and has never been saved. Even at the time of decision, it is difficult for a child to admit that nothing has changed when the teacher is happily telling him that he is born again. He will have a tendency to feel that this just doesn't work for him, or he will feel that everybody else's decision is like his and religion is just a game people play. These attitudes may close his mind to the truth.

It is better for the teacher to sow the seed, cultivate it, and be sensitive to the development and response of each child as to when it is time for salvation. It is also important that children sit with their parents and listen to the pastor's sermon every Sunday. This often is the "safest" time for the child to be saved. He can respond without peer pressure or teacher pressure.

If the teacher has properly sown the seed and the preacher preaches clear, simple salvation messages, children usually will be saved by the age of ten or twelve, and sometimes earlier.

Are there many plans (ways) of salvation?

Quickly we would say there is only one way to be born again. If the requirements for salvation are equal for all people, is this true for children also? Yes, the Bible is clear. There are certain basic requirements for all. When relating to the topic of salvation, the Bible is full of words such as, "all," "anyone," "everyone," "whoever."

For a person to be saved (child or adult) there are five basic requirements.

1. Hear the Gospel message. (John 5:24, Romans 10:14, Acts 2:37)

It is understood that the word "hear" as used in these verses relates to:

> (1) People who are capable of understanding the Gospel message.
>
> (2) People who personally receive the message.
>
> (3) People who feel responsible in relationship to the message.

2. When hearing the Gospel message there must be an awareness of being a sinner.

A child is not accountable until he understands that he is a sinner for whom Christ died. Repentance is possible only when there is this understanding and awareness concerning sin.

3. Conviction is necessary.

Conviction follows hearing and awareness. In Acts 2:37, after Peter had preached about sin and the Savior, we read, *When the people heard this, they were deeply troubled and said to Peter and the other apostles, "What shall we do?"* A person must be disturbed—troubled about his sinful condition—before he can be saved.

4. Repentance is necessary.

Note Peter's response in Acts 2:38, *"Each one of you must turn away from his sins."* (Also see Luke 13:3,5; Acts 3:19, 17:3) ("Turn away from" means to repent of.)

Repentance of sin means that there must be some understanding of what sin is. (A child old enough to be born again can understand what sin is.) Repentance cannot be meaningful without an understanding of sin.

The sin that condemns is the same for the child as for the adult. (John 3:18) (It is true that the child may not be as hardened in his sinful position as the adult is.)

5. Receiving Christ as Savior and Lord by faith is necessary. (John 1:12, 3:15-16; 5:24; Mark 8:34; 10:17-27; Luke 9:57-62)

There must be a balance with the use of Scripture when talking about what it means to be born again. The deeper meaning of John 3:16; 1:12; 5:24 is illustrated by Christ in Luke 9:57-62 and Mark 10:17-27. In the passages from Luke and Mark, Jesus tells of the cost, the demands, the responsibilities of becoming a disciple. He shared this with people before they made a decision. Some did not follow Him when they understood the responsibilities of being a disciple. Jesus did not make it easy in order to get decisions.

We must move from a "cheap grace" concept of salvation that often comes with a shallow interpretation of verses such as John 3:16, 1:12, and 5:24. We must interpret those verses in light of the teachings of Christ found in Mark 10:17-27 and Luke 9:57-62. The result will be a full Gospel picture, perhaps with fewer "decisions" but more disciples. This means that receiving Christ is more than raising a hand or praying a prayer.

Genuine saving faith must involve receiving Christ as Savior, but also as Lord. This means a surrender of one's life to follow Jesus in changing the world.

As long as a teacher's view of salvation includes only going to heaven and feeling happy, a complete view of salvation will not be taught to the children. And a complete view of salvation must be taught if we expect true disciples of Jesus.

Conclusion

Children are too important to be taken lightly. Children will be saved when they meet the Bible requirements for salvation.

The home and church have the responsibility to teach children.

The Holy Spirit is the one to convince, convict, and convert children.

It is easier for children to respond to Christ because they have not established a long lifetime pattern of resistance. Therefore, we must lead children into truth so that genuine, intelligent decisions can be made.

Chapter 21

CAN I LOSE MY SALVATION AFTER I AM BORN AGAIN?

A person does not become perfect or without sin when he is born again. While sin no longer dominates his life, he still will face temptation and sometimes will sin. The question that bothers some new and even some more mature believers is, "Can I lose my salvation?" If a person thinks that he may lose his salvation whenever he sins, he cannot have true joy, peace, or hope.

What does the Bible teach about this subject?

The Bible teaches that when a person is born again he cannot lose his salvation. Please study the following promise of Jesus to His followers.

"I am telling you the truth: whoever hears my words and believes in him who sent me has eternal life. He will not be judged, but has already passed from death to life." John 5:24

If a person hears the gospel and truly believes in Christ as his personal Savior and Lord, Jesus says that he has eternal life. **Has** is present tense; it is now—not to begin in the future. If the life he has is **eternal**, it is without end. This promise of Jesus is enough for us to believe in the security of the believer.

There are other verses where Jesus speaks of eternal life. John 3:15-16; John 8:12; 10:28; 1 John 5:13

When a person is born again, he has eternal life. In John 10:28-30 Jesus said, *"I give them eternal life, and they shall never die. No one can snatch them away from me. What my Father has given me is greater than everything, and no one can snatch them away from the Father's care. The Father and I are one."*

In Romans 8:35, 37-39 Paul says: *Who, then, can separate us from the love of Christ? Can trouble do it, or hardship or persecution or hunger or poverty or danger or death? No, in all these things we have complete victory through him who loved us! For I am certain that nothing can separate us from his love: Neither death nor life, neither angels nor heavenly rulers or powers, neither the present nor the future, neither the world above nor the world below—there is nothing in all creation that will ever be able to separate us from the love of God which is ours through Christ Jesus our Lord.*

From those verses it is very clear that once a person is born again, he cannot lose his salvation.

Let us look at the question in another way. When we were born again we became a part of God's family. In John 1:12 we read: *Some, however, did receive him and believed in him; so he gave them the right to become God's children.*

Once you were born physically, you became a part of a family. You had a father and mother. If as a young child you did something wrong or were disobedient, does this mean that you are no longer the child of your father and mother? No! Good or bad, you remain their child. If you are rebellious, it will hurt your parents; it will make them sad, but you are still their child and they are still your parents. If days pass and you are not talking with your parents, does this mean that they are no longer your parents? No! The fellowship, happiness, and joy may be missing, but the relationship of parent-child continues. It is wrong and bad for a believer to sin against God. But if it happens, and it will, God does not disown His children. He is sad, but He is still their Heavenly Father.

For more study on this, read Psalms 51. Note that David had sinned greatly. In verse 12 David said, *Give me again the joy that comes from your salvation.* He did not ask for salvation to be restored; he asked for the joy to be restored. He, in spite of his sin, continued to be God's child, but the joy was missing.

Since a person cannot lose his salvation, it is necessary to be born again only one time. Salvation cannot be repeated. There can be many commitments and rededications but only one New Birth.

The fact that the believer has eternal life, never to be lost, does not mean that we have freedom to sin as much as we like. The security of eternal life is not to be used as a license to sin. A true Christian will never say, "I am sure of going to heaven, therefore I will sin as often as I want to." A true believer will not enjoy living in sin. He will feel guilty and uncomfortable. Because God's grace and mercy assures us of eternal life, we will desire to live for Him.

It is good to know without a doubt that we cannot lose our place in heaven. By God's grace, that place is reserved for us. We can face life day by day with joy, peace, and hope, always telling others how wonderful God is.

Chapter 22

SHOULD I TITHE?

What is a tithe? The practice of giving tithes and offerings is seen in both the Old and New Testaments.

In Genesis 14:20 the Bible says, *And Abram gave Melchizedek a tenth of all the loot he had recovered.* Abram was a great man of God. God blessed him and used him to establish a great nation. Abram tithed. Abram had a grandson named Jacob. After a great victory Jacob set up a memorial stone and said, *"This memorial stone which I have set up will be the place where you are worshiped, and I will give you a tenth of everything you give me."* Genesis 28:22

A tithe is ten percent of income. Tithing is only the beginning. Many believers give more than ten percent as God blesses them. The tithe is to be given to the local church.

Why should the believer tithe?

1. The believer should tithe because of the nature of God our Father, and Jesus our Savior and Lord.

The spirit of giving was born in the heart of God. From the beginning of creation God has been a giving God. He gave light, plants, animals, and life to man and woman. In Old Testament days He gave the Jewish nation privileges and responsibilities. He gave the Law to help guide men as they developed individually and socially. Finally, He gave His best—His only Son Jesus, to live and die so that lost humanity might have a chance to live eternally. The heart of the giving nature of God is seen in John 3:16, *For God loved the world so much that he gave his only Son, so that everyone who believes in him may not die but have eternal life.*

Because our God is a God who loves and gives, we as His children will naturally desire to follow His example. Our love for God can be measured by our giving habits. When talking about Christian giving, Paul said, *...I am trying to find out how real your own love is. You know the grace of our Lord Jesus Christ; rich as he was, he made himself poor for your sake, in order to make you rich by means of his poverty.* 2 Corinthians 8:8-9

2. The believer should tithe because he has received so much.

Paul said, *You are so rich in all you have: in faith, speech, and knowledge, in your eagerness to help and in your love for us. And so we want you to be generous also in this service of love.*
2 Corinthians 8:7

All who have been born again have been blessed greatly. The believer has eternal life. God gives daily blessings, both material and spiritual. To receive generously and not give generously is ingratitude and selfishness. Tithing is a basic way God has planned for his children to demonstrate their love and appreciation.

3. The believer should tithe because he needs a regular reminder that all of his life and possessions belong to God.

...You do not belong to yourselves but to God. 1 Corinthians 6:19

The world and all that is in it belong to the Lord; the earth and all who live on it are his. Psalm 24:1

All we have belongs to the Lord. When we invited Christ into our lives as Savior and Lord, we ceased to be the lord of our lives.

Christ is Lord and King. This means that He controls our present and future. He is Lord of our children, house, land, work, and pleasure. One hundred percent belongs to God. He asks that we give back a tenth every week so that we will always be reminded that He is owner of all.

Because of this need to always be reminded of God's ownership, Paul said, *Every Sunday each one of you must put aside some money...* 1 Corinthians 16:2. Paul is talking about a regular offering given every Sunday. When we remember that all belongs to God, we will be more careful how we live and how we run our business. We will be more careful how we use the ninety percent remaining in our possession. God is concerned about the ten percent (tithe), but He is also concerned about how we use the ninety percent.

4. The believer should tithe because the Bible says he should.

Note that Paul uses the word **must** in the following verse. *Every Sunday each one of you must put aside some money...*
1 Corinthians 16:2

In Malachi 3:10 the Bible says, *Bring the full amount of your tithes to the Temple...*

Jesus commands tithing in Matthew 23:23; *You give to God one tenth even of the seasoning herbs, such as mint, dill, and cumin, but you neglect to obey the really important teachings of the Law, such as justice and mercy and honesty. These you should practice, without neglecting the others.*

5. The believer should tithe because this is God's plan to finance the work of the church.

When speaking about Christian giving Paul said, *For this service you perform not only meets the needs of God's people, but also produces an outpouring of gratitude to God.* 2 Corinthians 9:12 Also in 1 Corinthians 16:2 Paul says, *Every Sunday each of you must put aside some money, in proportion to what he has earned, and save it up, so that there will be no need to collect money when I come.* In Malachi 3:10 we read, *Bring the full amount of your tithes to the Temple, so that there will be plenty of food there.*

With tithes and offerings, a church is able to pay a pastor's salary, buy Bibles, build a chapel, help members who have special needs, and send out people to share the Good News in other places.

6. The believer should tithe because if he does not, he not only robs God, but also robs himself of many blessings.

I ask you, is it right for a person to cheat God? Of course not, yet you are cheating me. 'How?' you ask. In the matter of tithes and offerings. A curse is on all of you because the whole nation is cheating me. Bring the full amount of your tithes to the Temple, so that there will be plenty of food there. Put me to the test and you will see that I will open the windows of heaven and pour out on you in abundance all kinds of good things. Malachi 3:8-10

Remember that the person who plants few seeds will have a small crop; the one who plants many seeds will have a large crop. Each one should give, then, as he has decided, not with regret or out of a sense of duty; for God loves the one who gives gladly. And God is able to give you more than you need, so that you will always have all you need for yourselves and more than enough for every good cause. As the scripture says, "He gives generously to the needy; his kindness lasts forever." And God, who supplies seed for the sower and bread to eat, will also supply you with all the seed you need and will make it grow and produce a rich harvest from your generosity. He will always make you rich enough to be generous at all times... 2 Corinthians 9:6-11

Now back to the question, should I tithe?

If you are a believer, you are to tithe. Note **each** and **must** in the following verses. *Each one of you should give...* 2 Corinthians 9:7. Also in 1 Corinthians 16:2, *Every Sunday each of you must put aside some money...*

The answer is clear. Every believer must tithe if he is to be an obedient follower of Christ. Every believer must tithe if he is to know the unlimited riches of God. Children should be led to tithe faithfully from their allowances or earnings. "Every" includes the rich and the poor, the young and the old. (In some underdeveloped countries, the tithe may be in cash or in produce or animals.) Some say they are too poor to tithe. A reading of 2 Corinthians chapters 8 and 9 will show that believers are poor because they do not tithe. God promises to bless those who tithe. A tither will never be a beggar. The Bible speaks clearly about the great material and spiritual blessings awaiting those who give freely. The believer does not tithe in order to gain wealth, but when the believer gives out of a heart of love, God promises blessings as a result.

Please read the following Scripture references concerning tithing:

2 Corinthians 8-9; Malachi 3

Chapter 23

WHAT DOES THE BIBLE TEACH ABOUT COMMUNION?

Communion (Lord's Supper) and baptism are the two ordinances of the church. An ordinance is an order or a command. Concerning the Lord's Supper, Jesus said, "Do this..." Concerning baptism Jesus said, "Baptize them..."

These ordinances do not bring salvation or cleansing. If they are able to cleanse or bring salvation, there was no need for the death of Christ. Salvation and forgiveness of sin comes through faith in Christ. Salvation is found in Him alone and not in the waters of baptism or juice or bread used in the Lord's Supper. There is no salvation in external rituals or ceremonies.

Since these ordinances are not channels of grace or salvation, they are not to be called sacraments. A sacrament is not a Bible concept. Sacrament refers to a thing, ceremony, or ritual that can bring salvation to a person. Bible believers should not use the word sacrament to describe the Lord's Supper or baptism.

Concerning salvation and external ceremonies, Paul said in Philippians 3:3b-4,6-9, *We do not put any trust in external ceremonies. I could, of course, put my trust in such things. If anyone thinks he can trust in external ceremonies, I have even more reason to feel that way...As far as a person can be righteous by obeying the commands of the Law, I was without fault. But all those things that I might count as profit I now reckon as loss for Christ's sake. Not only those things; I reckon everything as complete loss for the sake of what is so much more valuable, the knowledge of Christ Jesus my Lord. For his sake I have thrown everything away; I consider it all as mere garbage, so that I may gain Christ and be completely united with him. I no longer have a righteousness of my own, the kind that is gained by obeying the Law. I now have the righteousness that is given through faith in Christ, the righteousness that comes from God and is based on faith.*

It is clear that salvation is not gained through external rituals or ceremonies.

What then is the meaning of the Lord's Supper?

In 1 Corinthians 11:23-29 we read: *For I received from the Lord the teaching that I passed on to you: that the Lord Jesus, on the night he was betrayed, took a piece of bread, gave thanks to God, broke it, and said, "This is my body, which is for you. Do this in memory of me." In the same way, after the supper he took the cup and said, "This cup is God's new covenant, sealed with my blood. Whenever you drink it, do so in memory of me." This means that every time you eat this bread and drink from this cup you proclaim the Lord's death until he comes. It follows that if anyone eats the Lord's bread or drinks from his cup in a way that dishonors him, he is guilty of sin against the Lord's body and blood. So then, everyone should examine himself first, and then eat the bread and drink from the cup. For if he does not recognize the meaning of the Lord's body when he eats the bread and drinks from the cup, he brings judgment on himself as he eats and drinks.*

The Lord's Supper is only for those who have been born again and have followed the Lord's teachings concerning baptism.

From the above it is clear that the Lord's Supper is a **memorial service**. Jesus said regarding the cup, "Whenever you drink it, do so in **memory** of me." He said the same thing about the bread.

The cup is a symbol of the shed blood of Jesus on the cross.

The bread is a symbol of the broken body of Jesus on the cross. These two elements, the juice and the bread, are symbolic, or pictures. The bread is not the actual body of Christ. The juice is not the actual blood of Christ. Jesus does not die every week. For a full understanding of this, read the book of Hebrews in the New Testament. Common phrases in that book concerning the death of Christ are: "Once for all," "Never to be repeated."

Jesus called Himself the "door," "the light," "the path," "the water," "the bread of life." John the Baptist called Him the "lamb of God."

These terms were used symbolically. He is the "door" to heaven—but He is more than a literal wooden door. He is the "light" but He is more than a bulb. He is the "path" that leads to heaven, but He is more than a dirt trail. He is the "bread" of life, but He is more than bread eaten by men. He often used earthly language to teach spiritual truths.

The Lord's Supper is a time when believers are made to remember the death of Christ as the sacrifice for their sins.

It is also a time to remember that the same Jesus who died on the cross is coming back again, not as Savior but as Ruler over believers and Judge of those who are unbelievers.

Chapter 24

WHAT DOES THE BIBLE TEACH CONCERNING HOMOSEXUALITY?

The first Biblical record of homosexuality is in Genesis 19:4-5.

Before the guests went to bed, the men of Sodom surrounded the house. All the men of the city, both young and old, were there. They called out to Lot and asked, "Where are the men who came to stay with you tonight? Bring them out to us!" The men of Sodom wanted to have sex with them.

In Genesis 18:20 we read the words of God describing Sodom and Gomorrah, *There are terrible accusations against Sodom and Gomorrah, and their sin is very great.*

God destroyed the two cities because of their sinfulness.

The Bible declares in Leviticus 18:22, *No man is to have sexual relations with another man; God hates that.*

In the New Testament we find Scriptures concerning homosexuality. In Romans 1:18-19, 21-28 the Bible says, *God's anger is revealed from heaven against all the sin and evil of the people whose evil ways prevent the truth from being known. God punishes them...* Verse 21, *...their thoughts have become complete nonsense, and their empty minds are filled with darkness. They say they are wise, but they are fools; instead of worshipping the immortal God, they worship images made to look like mortal man or birds or animals or reptiles. And so God has given those people over to do the filthy things their hearts desire, and they do shameful things with each other. They exchange the truth about God for a lie; they worship and serve what God has created* *instead of the Creator himself, who is to be praised forever! Amen. Because they do this, God has given them over to shameful passions. Even the women pervert the natural use of their sex by unnatural acts. In the same way the men give up natural sexual relations with women and burn with passion for each other. Men do shameful things with each other, and as a result they bring upon themselves the punishment they deserve for their wrongdoing. Because those people refuse to keep in mind the true knowledge about God, he has given them over to corrupted minds, so that they do the things that they should not do.*

Read again the above verses from the Bible. As you read, note that there is a relationship between worship and sin. Of course, this kind of worship is false worship that leaves an emptiness which allows a person to fall to the depths of sin. That sin is pictured in these verses as homosexuality involving both men and women. In verse 28 we see that those who practice such evil will bring punishment upon themselves. This punishment can be seen in many areas of life. There is alienation, shame, rejection, sexually transmitted diseases, and more.

In 1 Timothy 1:9-10 we read: *It must be remembered, of course, that laws are made, not for good people, but for law-breakers and criminals, for the godless and sinful, for those who are not religious or spiritual, for those who kill their fathers or mothers, for murderers, for the immoral, for sexual perverts, for kidnappers, for those who lie and give false testimony or who do anything else contrary to sound doctrine.*

Sexual perverts are listed among criminals, murderers, godless, and sinful.

Will a homosexual go to heaven?

From the Bible we find clear answers.

Revelation 21:8, *But cowards, traitors, perverts, murderers, the immoral, those who practice magic, those who worship idols, and all liars—the place for them is the lake burning with fire and sulfur, which is the second death.*

1 Corinthians 6:9-11, *Surely you know that the wicked will not possess God's Kingdom. Do not fool yourselves; people who are immoral or who worship idols or are adulterers or homosexual perverts or who steal or are greedy or are drunkards or who slander others or are thieves—none of these will possess God's Kingdom. Some of you were like that. But you have been purified from sin; you have been dedicated to God; you have been put right with God by the Lord Jesus Christ and by the Spirit of our God.*

There are clear truths seen in these portions of God's Word.

1. Homosexuality is abnormal. It is contrary to the will of God.

2. Homosexuality is the fruit of a religious perversion.

3. Homosexuality places a person outside the true community of God—here on earth and after death.

4. Homosexuality is to be discouraged and condemned.

5. Homosexuality destroys a person's sense of dignity and proper community relationships.

Is there hope for a homosexual?

Yes! It is not an unforgivable sin. The Scripture given earlier pictures the person who **continues** a homosexual life style as the one without hope of heaven. While the mind of the homosexual is extremely warped and twisted, true repentance can bring change to his life.

As shown in 1 Corinthians 6:11 (page 97) God can change the nature of a homosexual. But the person must be tired of his sin and want a genuine change before even God will help him to change.

Believers have a responsibility to hate sin in any form and this includes homosexuality. But believers have the responsibility to love homosexuals and desire to help them.

What is a homosexual to do if he wants help?

He should seek counseling. Often the pastor can help at this point, although professional Christian counseling may be best.

The first and greatest need of a homosexual is to repent, leaving his selfish desires, and accept Christ as the Lord of his life—including his sexual life. A genuine new birth will bring change to the homosexual.

After the new birth experience, there are three practical areas of life that should be seriously worked on.

1. A New Image of Self
The old destructive image is pictured in Galatians 5:16-21. The new image which must be cultivated is seen in Galatians 5:22-26. The old and new are also seen in Ephesians 2:1-10.

2. A New Appearance
If a person acts and dresses like a homosexual, he should try to change this. A man should act and dress like a man; a woman should act and dress like a woman. (Many homosexuals do not reveal their condition through obvious external appearances.)

3. A New Circle of Friends
A homosexual who has been born again must begin to develop friendships with people who are following Christ. He must develop friendships with non-homosexuals. He may not be able to

continue any friendships with homosexuals until he is himself completely victorious over the problem. Then he may help others to be free also.

What about homosexuals in the church?

Practicing homosexuals cannot fit into the body or fellowship of the local church. (You may want to read the Bible passages again concerning this subject.)

Practicing homosexuals should never be allowed to hold a position of leadership in the church. Only a sin-sick society will allow a practicing homosexual to act as pastor or priest. A homosexual can be deadly when mingling with church members. Children can be emotionally scarred for a lifetime by the advances and activity of a homosexual.

A homosexual who repents and has a new life style is something quite different. He should be treated like any other member of the church. By "practicing homosexual" we mean someone who **continues** in his life style of perversion.

Believers are to love all people. But believers are not to condone or in any way encourage homosexuality. The homosexual is to be pitied and encouraged to repent.

Chapter 25

IS IT WRONG TO DRINK ALCOHOLIC BEVERAGES AND SMOKE CIGARETTES?

What is included in alcoholic beverages? Anything which is consumed as a beverage that has alcohol in it. This includes such drinks as beer, wine, gin, etc.

Some have asked the question, "Can we continue to drink beer if we are born again?" Others have asked, "What is wrong with drinking or smoking?"

1. To follow Christ means that a person must surrender everything to the Lordship of Christ.

This **everything** means that all things in our lives must be surrendered to Christ. The real question is not, "Can I continue to drink?" The question is a much more serious one. It is, "Am I willing to turn all of my life over to the control of the Lord Jesus?" The real problem is not drinking. The problem is a desire to play god of life. The person who is not willing to let God be the God of all his life is choosing to play god—and destruction and loss is sure to follow. His family will suffer here and in eternity. To be saved—to gain salvation, a person must be willing to trust his life to Christ and must be willing to publicly acknowledge Christ as Lord. The Bible says, *If you confess that Jesus is Lord and believe that God raised him from death, you will be saved.* Romans 10:9. Not only must a person be willing to surrender his beer and cigarettes, he must be willing to let Christ become Lord of his work, his family, his recreation, his money, and all he has or hopes to have. The word LORD means ruler, boss.

A person cannot willfully retain lordship of any part of his life and at the same time receive Christ as Lord of his life. If a person says he must do as he pleases concerning drinking, he is not ready to be born again. It is sad that many choose to put beer in a higher position than Christ in their lives. Those who have completely surrendered their lives to Christ will have power to overcome drinking.

2. The principle of Lordship (ownership) influences all of life.

Once Jesus lives in our lives as Lord, we will reevaluate all we do and think. We will want to please Him and bring glory and honor to Him in every part of our lives. Concerning the believer's body, Paul said, *You know that your bodies are parts of the body of Christ... Don't you know that your body is the temple of the Holy Spirit, who lives in you and who was given to you by God? You do not belong to yourselves but to God; he bought you for a price. So use your bodies for God's glory.* 1 Corinthians 6:15, 19-20

The believer does not live a life of slavery to a list of do's and don'ts, but certain principles serve as guides in daily conduct.

One of these principles is:

Since the body is the temple of the Holy Spirit, it should be properly cared for. A believer should do nothing that will harm his body.

What about drinking alcoholic beverages?

More people die as a direct result of drinking than in all wars. This is seen in automobile accidents where innocent people often die. This is seen in fighting where people lose control of themselves and kill someone. It is seen in deaths from diseases caused by alcohol. Many kinds of diseases can be the direct result of drinking—diseases such as cancer, liver problems, stomach problems, and heart problems.

Some studies have revealed that one of every five people who take the first drink becomes an alcoholic. Lives are destroyed. Homes are destroyed. Children are made to suffer.

Is buying alcoholic drinks the best use of money? It is amazing that many people talk about how hard life is and how hard up they are and they still have money to buy a drink that destroys their bodies and sometimes their families.

The Bible has clear warnings to those who drink.

Show me people who drink too much, who have to try out fancy drinks, and I will show you people who are miserable and sorry for themselves, always causing trouble and always complaining. Their eyes are bloodshot, and they have bruises that could have been avoided. Don't let wine tempt you, even though it is rich red, and it sparkles in the cup, and it goes down smoothly. The next morning you will feel as if you had been bitten by a poisonous snake. Weird sights will appear before your eyes, and you will not be able to think or speak clearly. You will feel as if you were out on the ocean seasick, swinging high up in the rigging of a tossing ship. "I must have been hit," you will say; "I must have been beaten up, but I don't remember it. Why can't I wake up? I need another drink." Proverbs 23:29-35

Do not get drunk with wine, which will only ruin you... Ephesians 5:18.

The concluding questions concerning drinking alcoholic beverages may be: Is life enhanced? Is the body made more healthy? Does my family benefit? Is the church helped? Is Christ glorified and honored? The honest answer to all of these questions is a definite No!

What about smoking cigarettes?

All of the above statements about alcoholic beverages apply to smoking. The same principles apply. The believer is not to do any thing that will destroy his body or his good influence.

There is overwhelming opinion among medical experts that smoking destroys those who smoke and those nearby who breath the smoke. A congressional report from the United States says: "Each cigarette knocks about five minutes off the smoker's life. For an average smoker, that adds up to ten years." A British study reveals that 40 percent of smokers die before age 65 compared to only 15 percent of non-smokers.

Smoking is the leading cause of preventable diseases and premature death in the Western world, according to a U.S. surgeon general report on health consequences of cigarette smoking. A world health organization study reveals that someone dies every thirteen seconds due to smoking related diseases.

On the economic level, smokers file more disability claims and their absenteeism rate at work is 45 percent higher than non-smokers, and they tend to drink more alcohol.

In Japan, a recent study found that wives who do not smoke but who live with heavy smokers are twice as likely to die of lung cancer as wives of men who do not smoke. The same results were gathered in similar studies in Greece, West Germany, and the United States.

Again, the concluding questions should be asked: Does smoking enhance life? Does it make my body healthier? Does it improve my work on the job? Is it good for my children who breathe my smoke? Is it a wise use of my hard earned money? Does it help the church? Does it glorify and bring honor to Christ? Again, the answer is the same—No!

Why do people drink and smoke?

1. They have not completely yielded their lives to Christ.

2. They started for various reasons and got hooked. They became addicted. They became a slave to things that destroy their lives. Only those who decide to stop, recognize how deeply enslaved they are.

3. They have a fatalistic, hopeless view of life and just do not care. They live to live it up without purpose in life.

4. Some do these things out of ignorance. They are not educated concerning such matters.

5. Some smoke and drink because they think it is the smart thing to do. Television and magazines have falsely pictured these things as beautiful and as a sign of success.

6. Others do these things because they do not have enough strength and character to be different from the crowd.

THE ONLY SENSIBLE CONCLUSION IS TO NOT DRINK OR SMOKE!

It is not the right of a person to commit suicide, and that is what he is doing when he smokes or drinks.

It is not the right of a person to make his family suffer because of his smoking and drinking.

Destructive habits such as smoking, drinking, drugs, over-eating, etc., have no place in the life of a person guided by the principles of proper self-esteem, love for others, and love for the indwelling Holy Spirit. These principles are to serve as our guide on what we can do and what we should not do.

Chapter 26

WHAT DOES THE BIBLE SAY ABOUT SPEAKING IN UNKNOWN TONGUES?

Most of the books of the Bible do not mention speaking in unknown tongues. The subject is found only in a few passages in the New Testament. There are occasions where people spoke in other languages, but these were known tongues. Note some of these.

1. Acts 2:1-11
Many advocates of speaking in tongues use this passage as a basis for their beliefs. Look at the passage closely.

This was on the day of Pentecost. The tongues spoken of here were not unknown tongues. Many people were present from many different nations who spoke different languages. The Scripture says, *They were all filled with the Holy Spirit and began to talk in other languages, as the Spirit enabled them to speak. There were Jews living in Jerusalem, religious men who had come from every country in the world. When they heard this noise, a large crowd gathered. They were all excited, because each one of them heard the believers talking in his own language. In amazement and wonder they exclaimed, "These people who are talking like this are Galileans! How is it, then, that all of us hear them speaking in our own native languages?"* Acts 2:4-8

This was not speaking in "unknown tongues," but in tongues known by the people. The tongues were the native languages of the people who heard. No interpreter was necessary.

2. Acts 10:44-48
This was at Caesarea in the house of Cornelius, a Roman officer. Peter was preaching to a large group of unbelievers when the

Holy Spirit came down in a similar way as in Acts 2. In verse 47, Peter said, *"These people have received the Holy Spirit, just as we also did."* In Acts 11:15 Peter says, *"When I began to speak, the Holy Spirit came down on them just as on us at the beginning."* This was like the Pentecostal experience when people speaking different languages heard the message of Peter in their own language. Some Bible scholars say that these verses are to be interpreted as saying that when the people believed and were filled with the Holy Spirit, they began praising God in their own native tongue. This would be the most natural thing to do. It is natural for a person to revert to his national language when communing with God in a deep religious experience. For sure, this was not an unknown tongue.

3. Acts 18:24-19:6
At Ephesus Paul met some people who had only heard of the message and baptism of John the Baptist. They had not even heard about the Holy Spirit. Paul preached to them the message about Jesus and they gladly believed. After they believed they were baptized as followers of Christ. In their joy and excitement they began to speak in their native tongues as they praised God. (Ephesus was made up of people from many nations and many tongues.) Some of these languages were strange and even unknown to Paul. We can only guess that this was what happened. But we can be sure that this was not speaking in "unknown tongues." They proclaimed the message of God in human language. It did not cause division and strife between people as did the speaking in tongues in the Corinthian church. (You may want to read Acts 18:24-19:6 again.)

4. Tongues in the church at Corinth
Paul wrote to the Corinthian believers because there were so many problems in the church at Corinth. There are no records of unknown tongues in any of the other churches in the New Testament. There was no other church as weak as the church at Corinth. This church should not serve as an example for any church

to follow. Look at some of the problems, one of which was speaking in tongues.

Chapter 1 - filled with divisions, filled with quarrels
Chapter 3 - "You still live as the people of this world."
Chapter 4 - "Some of you have become proud."
Chapter 5 - "There is sexual immorality among you so terrible that not even the heathen would be guilty of it." "It is not right for you to be proud."
Chapter 6 - lawsuits against fellow Christians in heathen courts, immorality, permissiveness - "I am allowed to do anything."
Chapter 7 - marriage problems—unfaithfulness
Chapter 10 - danger of close connections to idol worship
Chapter 11 - turning the Lord's Supper into a feast and drinking party
Chapter 12 - misunderstanding concerning the gifts of the Spirit
Chapter 14 - disorder in the church services

Speaking in unknown tongues was a big problem in the church at Corinth. It produced pride, confusion, and division.

Paul does not encourage speaking in tongues. Rather, he discouraged the practice. Note some of his words in 1 Corinthians, chapters 12, 13 and 14.

After listing some of the gifts of the Spirit, he says, *Set your hearts, then, on the more important gifts. Best of all, however, is the following way.* (12:31) Paul then talks about love in chapter 13, the great love chapter of the Bible. He says, *Love is eternal. There are inspired messages, but they are temporary; there are gifts of speaking in strange tongues, but they will cease...* (13:8) Many Bible scholars believe speaking in tongues has ceased as the church has developed beyond its infant stage. We should remember that this letter to the Corinthians was among the very first of Paul's writings. Only the letters to the Thessalonians were written earlier. As far as Paul's writings are concerned, the experience of speaking in tongues ceased after the writing of 1 Corinthians. He did not mention speaking in tongues in his second letter to the Corinthian church or in any of his other writings to individuals or to churches.

Note further comments of Paul concerning the use of tongues.

First Priority 1 Corinthians 14:1-6

It is love, then, that you should strive for. Set your hearts on spiritual gifts, especially the gift of proclaiming God's message. 14:1

In relationship to proclaiming God's message Paul said, *The one who speaks in strange tongues does not speak to others but to God, because no one understands him.* 14:2a

The one who speaks in strange tongues helps only himself, but the one who proclaims God's message helps the whole church. 14:4

So when I come to you, my brothers, what use will I be to you if I speak in strange tongues? Not a bit, unless I bring you some revelation from God or some knowledge or some inspired message or some teaching. 14:6

Value of Speaking in Tongues

In the same way, how will anyone understand what you are talking about if your message given in strange tongues is not clear? Your words will vanish in the air! 1 Corinthians 14:9

Since you are eager to have the gifts of the Spirit, you must try above everything else to make greater use of those which help to build up the church. 1 Corinthians 14:12

When you give thanks to God in spirit only, how can an ordinary person taking part in the meeting say "Amen" to your prayer of thanksgiving? He has no way of knowing what you are saying. Even if your prayer of thanks to God is quite good, the other person is not helped at all. 1 Corinthians 14:16-17

I thank God that I speak in strange tongues much more than any of you. But in church worship I would rather speak five words that can be understood, in order to teach others, than speak thousands of words in strange tongues. Do not be like children in your thinking, my brothers; be children so far as evil is concerned, but be grown up in your thinking. 1 Corinthians 14:18-20

Paul is not saying that he spoke in tongues in the same way the Corinthians were doing. He says, "but in church worship..." Paul probably was referring to occasions in his private prayer life when only the Spirit could interpret to God "groans" or deep feelings which he could not utter in normal human language. (Romans 8:26)

If, then, the whole church meets together and everyone starts speaking in strange tongues—and if some ordinary people or unbelievers come in, won't they say you are all crazy? But if everyone is proclaiming God's message when some unbeliever or ordinary person comes in, he will be convinced of his sin by what he hears. He will be judged by all he hears, his secret thoughts will be brought into the open, and he will bow down and worship God, confessing, "Truly God is here among you!" 1 Corinthians 14:23-25

Orderliness and peace in worship is God's way.

Paul says, *The gift of proclaiming God's message should be under the speaker's control, because God does not want us to be in disorder but in harmony and peace.* 1 Corinthians 14:32

Paul continues, *Everything must be done in a proper and orderly way.* 1 Corinthians 14:40

CONCLUSION

This gift was found only in the infant church. The church at Corinth was very weak and immature in faith. Unknown tongues is not seen in any of the other churches of the New Testament. The church at Corinth is not an example that should be followed today. The use of unknown tongues caused pride, division, and confusion among the Corinthian people. It did not help people to be saved. It did not build up the church. It did not bring glory to Jesus. It is interesting to note that speaking in unknown tongues or ecstatic utterances is common in primitive religions which do not even acknowledge God.

The gift of speaking in unknown tongues is not found in the lists of gifts in Romans 12:6-8 or in Ephesians 4:11. It is not mentioned in any of the other letters of Paul. It is not found in the writings of Peter, James, John, or the gospels of Matthew and Luke. There is no record of any apostles speaking in unknown tongues. There is no record of Jesus speaking in unknown tongues. He was filled with the Holy Spirit, (Luke 3:21,22; 4:1,14,18) but he did not speak in tongues. He did not teach others to do it.

Jesus commissioned his disciples, *Go, then, to all peoples everywhere and make them my disciples: baptize them in the name of the Father, the Son, and the Holy Spirit, and* **teach them to obey everything I have commanded you.** *And I will be with you always, to the end of the age.* Matthew 28:19-20

Chapter 27

WHAT AM I TO DO WHEN SOMEONE WRONGS ME?

It is natural for the unbeliever to become angry when someone wrongs him. It is natural to strike back or seek revenge. This is the way for a person who has not been born again. But the believer will have a new attitude. The true Christian does not live a life of bitterness and hatred toward others. Christ is the new Lord (ruler) when a person is born again. Christ becomes our pattern. We are to have His attitude toward others.

What does the Bible say about love and forgiveness?

You may say, "He said some very bad things about me and I just cannot love and forgive." On the cross they spat on Jesus, they thrust a spear into His side. They cursed Him, stripped Him, drove a nail into one hand and then into the other hand. His response was, *"Forgive them, Father! They don't know what they are doing."* Luke 23:34 The Bible says, *The attitude you should have is the one that Christ Jesus had.* Philippians 2:5

In Ephesians 4:31-32 we read: *Get rid of all bitterness, passion, and anger. No more shouting or insults, no more hateful feelings of any sort. Instead, be kind and tender-hearted to one another, and forgive one another, as God has forgiven you through Christ.*

From these verses we see that the basis for our being able to forgive is the fact that God has forgiven us. The believer is able to understand true forgiveness. Through the new birth we have new minds, thoughts and attitudes. Paul speaks of this in Ephesians 4:23-24: *Your hearts and minds must be made completely new, and you must put on the new self...*

You may say, "Yes, that is all true, but I just cannot forgive." You are right, **you** cannot; but with the help of Christ you can. Every believer should memorize Philippians 4:13, *I have the strength to face all conditions by the power that Christ gives me.*

WHAT SHOULD I DO WHEN SOMEONE WRONGS ME?

Remember that true worship requires forgiveness.

The verses below are from the Sermon on the Mount. This was the great message of Jesus to His followers.

So if you are about to offer your gift to God at the altar and there you remember that your brother has something against you, leave your gift there in front of the altar, go at once and make peace with your brother, and then come back and offer your gift to God. Matthew 5:23-24

From the Scripture we learn:

1. The true believer will worship.
2. Offering a gift is a normal part of worship.
3. When we come before God to worship, we will be reminded of our unforgiving spirit toward a brother.
4. We cannot really worship if there is an unforgiving spirit in our hearts.
5. We are to leave the place of worship and go make things right with our brother. This must be done without delay. It is not good enough to say, "later."
6. After things are settled with our brother, then we will want to come back and offer our gifts and worship to God.

Determine not to take revenge when someone wrongs me.

In Matthew 5:38-39 Jesus says, *"You have heard that it was said, 'An eye for an eye, and a tooth for a tooth.' But now I tell you: do not take revenge on someone who wrongs you. If anyone slaps you on the right cheek, let him slap your left cheek too."*

It is normal for the unbeliever to seek revenge. But it is not normal for the believer. We are not to repay; we are to love.

If someone has done you wrong, do not repay him with a wrong. Try to do what everyone considers to be good. Do everything possible on your part to live in peace with everybody. Never take revenge, my friends, but instead let God's anger do it. For the scripture says, "I will take revenge, I will pay back, says the Lord." Instead, as the scripture says: "If your enemy is hungry, feed him; if he is thirsty, give him a drink"... Romans 12:17-20

Love and pray for those who wrong you.

"You have heard that it was said, 'Love your friends, hate your enemies.' But now I tell you: love your enemies and pray for those who persecute you, so that you may become the sons of your Father in heaven. For he makes his sun to shine on bad and good people alike, and gives rain to those who do good and to those who do evil. Why should God reward you if you love only the people who love you? Even the tax collectors do that! And if you speak only to your friends, have you done anything out of the ordinary? Even the pagans do that!" Matthew 5:43-47

The pagans love those who are their friends. The believer loves his friends and his enemies. How do we know that we love our enemies? Jesus said, "Love and pray for your enemies." When we begin to pray that God will bless our enemies, we will know that we really love them.

So it is not enough just to love, we are also to pray that good things will happen to our enemies. *Ask God to bless those who persecute you—yes, ask Him to bless, not to curse.* Romans 12:14

Be able to pray as Jesus taught us to pray.

"This, then, is how you should pray: 'Our Father in heaven: May your holy name be honored; may your Kingdom come; may your will be done on earth as it is in heaven. Give us today the food we need. Forgive us the wrongs we have done, as we forgive the wrongs that others have done to us. Do not bring us to hard testing, but keep us safe from the Evil One.'" Matthew 6:9-13

From these verses we learn some great truths:
1. God is approached with great respect. He is recognized as Father, Holy, and King.
2. The believer desires that God's Kingdom become a reality even on earth, even in this life.
3. God's rule and will is more important than a person's food. (verses 10-11)
4. The believer acknowledges his own shortcomings and faults and asks forgiveness. (verse 12)
5. The believer is then able to forgive others who have wronged him. (verse 13)

I can choose a curse or a blessing.

"If you forgive others the wrongs they have done you, your Father in heaven will also forgive you. But if you do not forgive others, then your Father will not forgive the wrongs you have done." Matthew 6:14-15

1. A curse (v.15)
This verse clearly states that if you will not forgive others when they wrong you, God will not forgive your sins. Many people are tired and frustrated because they continue to carry their own personal unforgiven sins. They do this because they refuse to forgive someone who has done something wrong to them. This can lead to mental sickness and emotional breakdown.

2. A Blessing (v.14)
The blessing is the freedom and peace that comes when God has forgiven a person of all his wrong doings. This will come only after a person has cleared up all his bad feelings of bitterness and hatred toward someone who has done him wrong. Only then can a believer take his sins to God and find forgiveness.

Conclusion

What am I to do when someone does something wrong to me?
What am I to do when someone says something untrue about me?
What am I to do when someone wants to hurt me?

There is no question about what the true believer should do. We must love and forgive and pray for that person. This will not be easy, but with God's help we can do it. We are able to do it because we are special people of God. *You are the people of God; he loved you and chose you for his own. So then, you must clothe yourselves with compassion, kindness, humility, gentleness, and patience. Be tolerant with one another and forgive one another whenever any of you has a complaint against someone else. You must forgive one another just as the Lord has forgiven you.* Colossians 3:12-13

The genuine believer does not have a choice. If we have the nature of Christ in us, we must love and forgive.

BUT WHAT DO I DO NOW?

1. Confess to God that you are a sinner and in need of help. Humility is always the best starting point.

2. Ask God to forgive you for having a hateful spirit toward another person. Even if you have done nothing bad to that person, you are guilty of hating him for what he has done to you.

3. Ask God to help you love that person.

4. Ask God to give you wisdom and love as you go to the person.

5. In humility and love, go to the person and say, "I am sorry that I have had a bad, unforgiving spirit toward you. Please forgive me."

You may say, "But isn't this weakness on my part? He is the one who should be coming to me." No, it is not weakness. It is the strength that comes from Christ living within you. Perhaps the one who offended you was not aware of what he was doing. Maybe if he is aware, he is not strong enough to admit his fault.

So, be strong, be victorious, be the one to initiate the reconciliation. Everyone will be blessed by your action. You will be glad you did.

Other Scriptures to read on this subject:

Matthew 18
1 Corinthians 13

Chapter 28

WHAT IS A CHRISTIAN MARRIAGE?

Christian marriage is possible only for those who have been born again. It is Christ in the marriage that makes it Christian. Only when Christ is Savior and Lord of both husband and wife can a Christian marriage exist.

Marriage is the foundation for the development of the home. If the foundation is weak, the home will be weak. Christ must be an essential part of the marriage relationship if the home is to be a Christian home. Many people think they have a Christian home even though, in reality, Christ is not the head of the home.

A Christian marriage must recognize the Bible as the guide in all things in the home. The Bible must supersede cultural traditions whenever there is a contradiction.

Non-Biblical views of marriage are common.

1. For some, marriage is a 1 + 1 = 2 relationship.

This is a his and her relationship. He has his world to live in, his things, and she has her world and her things. Their careers are often unrelated. Each claims their money as their own to use as they please. It is like two railroad tracks going on forever, so close but always maintaining a distance. Close, but never blending as one.

2. Another non-Biblical view of marriage is 1 + 1 = 3.

It is the husband and wife and a third party. The third party may be in-laws or a boyfriend or girlfriend. The inability of a person to cut the strings with parents is one of the most damaging aspects of many marriages.

What is the Christian view of marriage?

1 + 1 = 1 is the proper formula for a Christian marriage.

For this reason a man will leave his father and mother and unite with his wife, and the two will become one. Ephesians 5:31

The two will become one. This involves all aspects of life. The two become more than either could ever become without the other. It is not a matter of sacrificing; it is a matter of becoming all God wants a person to be through a relationship with the mate.

This triangle helps in understanding the key relationships in Christian marriage.

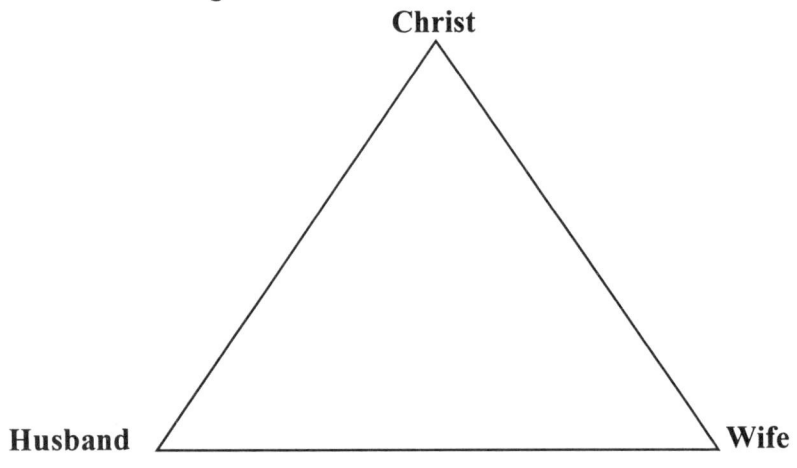

```
           Christ
            /\
           /  \
          /    \
         /      \
        /        \
       /          \
      /            \
Husband ―――――――――― Wife
```

Husband and wife share their lives with each other—the weaknesses and the strengths. The husband is related to Christ, who gives him strength to become the best Christian husband possible. In the same way the wife relates to Christ and from that relationship gains self-hood and dignity. As both husband and wife become more like Christ, they share this kind of new life with each other. Each is able to love the other properly because each has been loved properly by Christ.

This is Christian marriage. Children find security and warmth inside the triangle. They are aware of the special relationships as they grow up. They will know the value of a Christian home and will try to duplicate it in their own marriages.

Let us now look at some key areas of life that must be dealt with by every husband and wife. Please take time to do the marriage check-up and then we will discuss each of the four areas briefly.

MARRIAGE CHECK-UP

1. How long did you know each other before marriage? ____

2. Did your parents approve of your marriage? Strongly ____ Mildly ____ Disapproved ____ Strongly disapproved ____

3. Do you consider your parents' economic condition as:
A. Upper class ____ B. Middle class ____ C. Lower class ____

4. What is your education attainment? College ____ High School ____ Elementary School ____

===

1. IN-LAWS
   (1) Do you feel comfortable when you are with your in-laws? Yes ____ No ____
   (2) Do you resent your mate going to the house of his/her parents? Yes ____ No ____
   (3) Does your mate spend too much time with parents? Yes ____ No ____
   (4) Do your in-laws interfere too much in your family? Yes ____ No ____
   (5) Do you and your mate argue about in-laws? Yes ____ No ____

2. <u>RELIGION</u>
   (1) Do you agree on basic Bible doctrines?
             Yes ___ No ___
   (2) Do you pray with your mate? Yes ___ No ___
   (3) Do you attend church with your mate?
             Yes ___ No ___
   (4) Do you argue over the way your children should be disciplined?   Yes ___ No ___
   (5) Have you and your mate talked about God's purpose for life and how the two of you fit into that plan?
             Yes ___ No ___

3. <u>MONEY</u>
   (1) Do you feel pressure and tension because of finances?
     A. Daily ___ B. Often ___ C. Rarely ___
   (2) Does your mate waste too much money?
             Yes ___ No ___
   (3) Do you follow a budget when spending money?
             Yes ___ No ___
   (4) Do you have arguments over money?
             Yes ___ No ___
     If yes: Heated ___ Mild ___ Friendly ___
   (5) Do you consider your earnings as yours to use as you please, and his earnings for him to use as he pleases?
             Yes ___ No ___

4. <u>SEX</u>
   (1) As you were growing up, did you think that sex was dirty and bad?   Yes ___ No ___
   (2) How do you now view sex?
     A. Duty ___ B. Expression of love ___
     C. Self-satisfaction ___ D. To be endured ___
   (3) Does your mate understand your sexual feelings?
             Yes ___ No ___

(4) Do you have disagreements about sex?
   A. Often ___   B. Sometimes ___   C. Rarely ___
   A. Heated ___ B. Mild ___   C. Easily talked out ___
(5) Are you jealous?
   A. Often ___   B. Seldom ___   C. Never ___
(6) Do you have arguments over jealousy?
   Strong ___   Mild ___

===

In-laws

In the story of creation, after God created Adam and Eve, He said, *That is why a man leaves his father and mother and is united with his wife, and they become one.* Genesis 2:24

When two people get married they should leave their father and mother. This does not suggest that honor and respect for parents should cease. It is clear, though, that one house is not big enough for two families—parents and their married children—if each family is to achieve maximum development and happiness.

Religion

It is important that husband and wife share the same religion. If there is division at this point, it is difficult for other areas of life to work out well. The Bible says, *Do not try to work together as equals with unbelievers, for it cannot be done. How can right and wrong be partners? How can light and darkness live together? How can Christ and the Devil agree? What does a believer have in common with an unbeliever?* 2 Corinthians 6:14-15

If one of the mates is born again, he is to seek the salvation of the other. Only when both are born again can they claim to have a Christian home. When parents do not agree on religion it becomes very difficult for the children to have spiritual direction.

Money

A Christian couple will make wise use of the money God gives them. Money is to be mastered, it is not to be the master.

Some points to remember about financial success in the home:
1. Give the first tenth to God. (The Bible calls this a tithe.)
2. Prepare a budget and follow it.
3. Live within your income. Over extension is when a person spends more than he has coming in. This will cause great tension in the marriage relationship.
4. Do not try to start on the same level of living as that of your parents. It took them many years to get where they are.
5. The husband and wife should discuss finances openly. Any major expenditure should be discussed and agreed upon.

Sex
A man should fulfill his duty as a husband, and a woman should fulfill her duty as a wife, and each should satisfy the other's needs. A wife is not the master of her own body, but her husband is; in the same way a husband is not the master of his own body, but his wife is. Do not deny yourselves to each other, unless you first agree to do so for a while in order to spend your time in prayer; but then resume normal marital relations. 1 Corinthians 7:3-5

There are two extreme views concerning sex that bring trouble to the marriage. One is the idea that sex is bad and is to be endured as a duty only. In many cultures this is more likely to be the idea of the woman than of the man. A person with this view cannot fully express love for the marriage partner. The second extreme view is that sex is basically a way for personal satisfaction. This is more common among men than among women. This view degrades sex and the spouse is treated as an object to be used for personal gratification. This is selfishness. It is not a way to express love.

Sex within marriage is a God-given gift. It is sacred. God gave the sexual relationship so that married people can say "I love you," in the most intimate way possible. It was given also that the earth would be populated; but it is more than that.

In conclusion, the following passage from the Bible is a beautiful summary of the marriage relationship.

Submit yourselves to one another because of your reverence for Christ. Wives, submit yourselves to your husbands as to the Lord. For a husband has authority over his wife just as Christ has authority over the church; and Christ is himself the Savior of the church, his body. And so wives must submit themselves completely to their husbands just as the church submits itself to Christ. Husbands, love your wives just as Christ loved the church and gave his life for it. He did this to dedicate the church to God by his word, after making it clean by washing it with water, in order to present the church to himself in all its beauty—pure and faultless, without spot or wrinkle or any other imperfection. Men ought to love their wives just as they love their own bodies. A man who loves his wife loves himself. (No one ever hates his own body. Instead he feeds it and takes care of it, just as Christ does the church; for we are members of his body.) As the Scripture says, "For this reason a man will leave his father and mother and unite with his wife, and the two will become one." There is a deep secret truth revealed in this scripture, which I understand as applying to Christ and the church. But it also applies to you: every husband must love his wife as himself, and every wife must respect her husband. Ephesians 5:21-33

When facing conflict in the four areas given in this study, it is important that husband and wife face the problems prayerfully. Some newly married people think that marriage will end all problems, but usually new and different problems arise. There will be conflicts in all four areas mentioned in this lesson, but the conflicts need not do damage to the marriage relationship. A great deal of listening, understanding, and flexibility is necessary in all marriage relationships. A man and woman can experience a Christian marriage and a lifetime of celebration when Christ is the head of the home.

Chapter 29

HOW AM I TO DISCIPLINE MY CHILDREN?

First it must be understood that children need to be disciplined.

It is the parents' responsibility to discipline their children.

Undisciplined children often become undisciplined adults.

Discipline involves: training;
correction;
punishment;
chastisement;
development;
cultivation.

What does the Bible say about discipline of children?

Love the Lord your God with all your heart, with all your soul, and with all your strength. Never forget these commands that I am giving to you today. Teach them to your children. Repeat them when you are at home and when you are away, when you are resting and when you are working. Deuteronomy 6:5-7

There are certain truths which parents are to teach their children. This means that parents must know what the Bible is teaching if they are to be of help in leading their children in the right direction. The above portion of Scripture tells us that teaching spiritual, Biblical truths is a full time job, everyday, everywhere in the family. Parents fail when they give this responsibility to the church.

Children, it is your Christian duty to obey your parents, for this is the right thing to do...Parents, do not treat your children in such a way as to make them angry. Instead, raise them with Christian discipline and instruction. Ephesians 6:1,4

From these verses we learn that:

1. Children are to obey their parents.

2. Parents should not try to make a child angry.

3. Parents are to raise their children with Christian discipline and instruction.

This means that parents are to lead their children in setting Bible standards of action and lead the children to an understanding and acceptance of Bible teachings.

Every parent has an obligation to learn the Word of God, not only for himself, but also for the welfare of his children. A father who never studies the Bible is failing to be the kind of father he should be.

Additional Scripture concerning discipline:

A wise son pays attention when his father corrects him.... If you don't punish your son, you don't love him. If you do love him, you will correct him. Proverbs 13:1,24

Teach a child how he should live, and he will remember it all his life...Children just naturally do silly, careless things, but a good spanking will teach them how to behave. Proverbs 22:6,15

Don't hesitate to discipline a child. A good spanking won't kill him. As a matter of fact, it may save his life. Proverbs 23:13-14

Correction and discipline are good for children. If a child has his own way, he will make his mother ashamed of him. Proverbs 29:15

Some helps in discipline:

1. The father and mother should agree on when and how to discipline a child.

2. Discipline must begin early.

3. Parents are to control the child. The child is not to control the parents.

How do children control parents? They throw a crying tantrum until they get their way. If the parent is weak, children know that if they cry loudly enough and long enough they will get their way. A child is rebelling against authority when he jumps up and down and screams. He must be stopped with firmness and authority. Violence and uncontrolled emotional outbursts will be more likely among adults and teens who were not trained to control their emotions when they were small children.

4. Discipline should be done in love.

The parent should not spank a child when the parent is angry. The parent should promise the spanking, then cool off. After the cooling off period, the parent should explain to the child again why the spanking is necessary and, with firmness, spank the child. A child properly disciplined will not need to be disciplined often. One good spanking is much better than many little pats that mean nothing. If you love him you will discipline him.

5. Healthy discipline must be firm.

To spank a child repeatedly with a newspaper only irritates. It does not discipline.

When the parent tells a child to do something, the child must do it. The parent should never tell a child to do something unless he expects the child to do it. If a child openly rebels and fails to do what the parent has told him to do, the parent must act with authority and firmness. The child must obey his parents at a very early age if he is to grow up as a healthy, law-abiding citizen.

6. How hard am I to spank a child?

Hard enough to make him do what you have instructed him to do (but not to cause injury). Punishment is not punishment unless there is pain. If parents tell a child not to play in the busy highway and the child fails to obey, the parent is to punish the child strongly enough that when the child thinks of playing in the highway again, he will remember the punishment and will not do it. This is effective discipline.

Discipline your children while they are young enough to learn. If you don't, you are helping them destroy themselves. Proverbs 19:18

Chapter 30

WHAT TITLES DO WE USE WHEN REFERRING TO RELIGIOUS LEADERS?

Jesus was talking to the crowds and to his disciples about the religious leaders of the day when He said, *"They do everything so that people will see them...They love the best places at feasts and the reserved seats in the synagogues; they love to be greeted with respect in the market places and to have people call them 'Teacher.' You must not be called 'Teacher,' because you are all brothers of one another and have only one Teacher. And you must not call anyone here on earth 'Father,' because you have only one Father in heaven. Nor should you be called 'Leader,' because your one and only leader is the Messiah. The greatest one among you must be your servant. Whoever makes himself great will be humbled, and whoever humbles himself will be made great."* Matthew 23:5-12

Jesus is clearly speaking against the misuse of religious titles. It is wrong to call a religious leader father, reverend, bishop, cardinal, pastor, or any other title unduly magnifying a person. Man is not to be glorified. Only Christ is worthy of our exaltation.

This does not mean that we do not respect religious leaders. We are to respect them as well as every other brother and sister in the faith.

People who demand respect and a special recognition are to be pitied. Their spirit is not that of Christ.

The work of the pastor is a God-given task and believers are to recognize that God has called certain men to do the work of the pastor. We are not to minimize this work, but the pastor should not be elevated above the church members by the use of titles.

In addition to the words of Jesus, what else does the Bible say about the use of titles for religious leaders?

"Brother" was the term used in the New Testament when referring to fellow believers. After Paul had been converted, he was referred to as "brother." In Acts 9:17 we read: *So Ananias went, entered the house where Saul was, and placed his hands on him. "Brother Saul," he said, "the Lord has sent me—Jesus himself..."*

Paul thought of himself as a brother to other followers of Christ. In 1 Corinthians 3:1, Paul says to the believers in Corinth, *As a matter of fact, my brothers...* Again he says in 1 Corinthians 14:6, *So when I come to you, my brothers...* In Philippians 2:29, Paul says concerning someone he is sending to the believers at Philippi, *Receive him, then, with joy, as a brother in the Lord. Show respect to all such people as he...* Throughout Paul's writings he uses the word "brother" to refer to other believers.

Paul himself was never addressed with a religious title. He was never called "Father Paul," or "Reverend Paul," or "Pastor Paul."

None of the disciples of Jesus used religious titles attached to their names. James was the pastor of the church in Jerusalem, but we do not read "Reverend James" in the Bible.

It is enough to say that the Bible does not teach or encourage the use of special titles for religious leaders. Jesus spoke against it.

Why is this important?

When Jesus made such an issue of religious titles in Matthew 23, He knew the danger of the use of such titles. A study of that chapter will reveal what the dangers are.

Jesus talked about the superiority feeling of those who enjoyed being called "Father," etc. Jesus saw the danger of pride that comes when a man begins to magnify himself by having people address him with special titles. He saw the danger of religious leaders losing touch with the common person's life. This often happens when there is a gap between the leaders and the members. This gap is made greater when one person is elevated so high above the common people.

The use of Brother in the New Testament and Today

Religious leaders in the New Testament used this term to refer to other believers. There was no danger in using the term because it tells of a special relationship between believers which is made possible because of Jesus Christ.

Today, when we use the word "brother" it describes a special relationship between believers. This special relationship is not something brought about by the goodness or accomplishments of the believers. There is nothing of which to boast except the new nature made possible by faith in Christ. So when a believer calls another believer "brother," it speaks of a relationship, and praise immediately goes to Jesus Christ, the source of the relationship.

For the one who understands this, there is no higher honor or respect—because we live to glorify Christ. To be addressed as Father or Reverend is a great insult to a person who chooses only to glorify One—Christ.

You may say, "The use of titles is cultural." The believer should not live according to cultural standards; rather he should live by the standards of the Word of God.

What do we call our pastor?

Among believers you call him by name or "Brother _____."

If you are among unbelievers, you may choose to call him "Mr. _____." (Only believers will understand and appreciate the Biblical term, "Brother." To use it among unbelievers is meaningless. Around the world "Mr." is an acceptable secular title of respect.)

If you are to introduce your pastor to a group of believers, you could say, "I introduce to you Brother Juan Reyes, who is doing the work of the pastor at the _____ Church."

This introduction reveals a special relationship that magnifies Christ, yet reveals and magnifies the gift of doing the work of a pastor.

If you introduce your pastor to a group of unbelievers you would say, "May I introduce Mr. Juan Reyes, pastor of _____ Church."

Conclusion

If we follow the Bible, we will ignore man-made religious pedestals and will not use religious titles. Hierarchies have no place in New Testament Christian religion. Such hierarchies have arisen when religious leaders demand high positions of praise that lead to uncontrolled power and the amassing of wealth at the expense of ordinary people. It is a joy to see a man humble enough that he does not demand special recognition. This man is truly free in Christ.

Chapter 31

WHAT IS A CHURCH?

Jesus Christ said, *"I will build my church, and not even death will ever be able to overcome it."* Matthew 16:18 Perhaps the greatest picture of the church is seen in the book of Ephesians. Paul describes the church as the living and powerful body of Christ.

A church has an organizational structure, but is much more than an organization.

A church cannot be brought to life or sustained by man, only by Christ.

A church is not only godly in its origin, but also in its future and purpose.

A church may meet in a place made by human hands, but the church is much more than the building where meetings are held.

When we speak of a church, it is recognized that we are talking about the New Testament concept of church. What is the New Testament concept?

THE CHURCH AS THE BODY OF CHRIST
(Based on Paul's letter to the Ephesians.)

1. The church is related to God's eternal plan.

God has an eternal plan for the universe and for all people. We read about it in Ephesians. *Even before the world was made, God had already chosen us to be his through our union with Christ, so that we would be holy and without fault before him. Because of his love God had already decided that through Jesus Christ he would make us his sons—this was his pleasure and purpose...In all his wisdom and insight God did what he had purposed, and made known to us the secret plan he had already decided to complete by means of Christ. This plan, which God will complete when the time is right, is to bring all creation together, everything in heaven and on earth, with Christ as head. All things are done according to God's plan and decision; and God chose us to be his own people in union with Christ because of his own purpose, based on what he had decided from the very beginning. Let us, then, who were the first to hope in Christ, praise God's glory!* Ephesians 1:4-5, 8-12

Also in Ephesians 3:9-11 we read: *God, who is the Creator of all things, kept his secret hidden through all the past ages, in order that at the present time, by means of the church, the angelic rulers and powers in the heavenly world might learn of his wisdom in all its different forms. God did this according to his eternal purpose, which he achieved through Christ Jesus our Lord.*

The idea of the church is not new; it is older than man's earthly history. It is a part of God's eternal plan for creation. Note in the previous verses the words **eternal**, **plan**, **purpose** and **by means of the church**. The church is essential in God's purpose. God knows where history is going. He knows where nations are going. He knows the beginning and the ending of man on earth. The church is a part of that plan.

2. Christ is the head of the church.

Christ rules there above all heavenly rulers, authorities, powers, and lords; he has a title superior to all titles of authority in this world and in the next. God put all things under Christ's feet and gave him to the church as supreme Lord over all things. The church is Christ's body, the completion of him who himself completes all things everywhere. Ephesians 1:21-23

Also in Colossians 1:18, *He is the head of his body, the church; he is the source of the body's life.* Christ is the originator, the designer, the architect of the church.

3. Christ is the source of the church's:

Pardon
Please take time to read Ephesians 2:1-10. Verse one says, *In the past you were spiritually dead because of your disobedience and sins.* Verse four says, *But God's mercy is so abundant...*

Peace
For Christ himself has brought us peace. Ephesians 2:14

Power
And how very great is his power at work in us who believe. This power working in us is the same as the mighty strength which he used when he raised Christ from death, and seated him at his right side in the heavenly world. Ephesians 1:19-20

4. The church is one body with many working parts.

One Body
Paul speaks of one body and the unity of that body. *Do your best to preserve the unity which the Spirit gives by means of the peace that binds you together. There is one body and one Spirit, just as there is one hope to which God has called you.* Ephesians 4:3-4

Paul encourages the believers to preserve the unity and gives the secret of how this can be done: *Be always humble, gentle, and patient. Show your love by being tolerant with one another.* Ephesians 4:2

Many working parts
Paul tells of this in Ephesians 4:7,16, *Each one of us has received a special gift in proportion to what Christ has given...Under his*

control all the different parts of the body fit together, and the whole body is held together by every joint with which it is provided. So when each separate part works as it should, the whole body grows and builds itself up through love.

5. Every member of the church has a special work to do as part of the total life of the church.

Concerning the church Paul says, *So when each separate part works as it should, the whole body grows and builds itself up through love.* Ephesians 4:16

What is a church?

It is God's family of believers. It is the fulfillment of the work of Christ—the body of Christ.

Are all people part of this family? No. The Bible says, *He came to his own country, but his own people did not receive him. Some, however, did receive him and believed in him; so he gave them the right to become God's children.* John 1:11-12

These verses indicate that some people are a part of the family and some are not. It also teaches that those who believe in him and receive him are counted as God's children. To be a part of the church, the body of Christ, one must believe in (trust in, rely upon) Jesus as Savior and Lord of his daily life.

THE LOCAL CHURCH
(As seen in the Acts of the Apostles)

There is no conflict in the views of the church as found in Ephesians and as found in Acts. Ephesians gives a telescopic view from above history, telling how all believers relate to Christ and the Kingdom of God. Acts gives a close-up microscopic view of a local (one geographical area) group of believers who are a part of the body of Christ. The book of Acts, as well as other books of the New Testament, gives primary attention to the local church —the church in action.

The same five truths regarding the church as the body of Christ also apply to the local church.

A local, New Testament-principled church is **related to eternity**. It is a part of God's plan for the universe. It is a group of believers who are commissioned to participate in increasing God's Kingdom through sharing their faith with unbelievers.

A local church recognizes **Christ as the head** of the group.

A local church understands that **Christ is the only source of pardon, peace and power**.

A local church experiences oneness or unity within the membership even though there is a variety of talents among the members.

A local church knows that all parts of the body—every member— must function, must do his part if the entire membership is to grow.

From a study of the first chapters of the Acts of the Apostles we see that a local church is:

A group of people who have turned from their sins to place full trust in Jesus as Savior and Lord. They are then baptized by immersion. These individuals continue to meet on a regular basis as members of the family of God. They will fellowship in prayer, praise, and Bible study for the definite purpose of glorifying Christ and expanding His Kingdom on earth. This is a church.

This group called a church is more than a social organization. It is special because:

1. The Holy Spirit of God brought the group together. The members of the group are "called out ones" with a special purpose. (A New Testament Greek word used to describe those who made up the early church is ekklesia, "called out ones.")

2. There is a special union among the members brought about by supernatural means. Koinonia is the Greek word that describes this special relationship among believers. It is Christian fellowship.

3. There is a common commitment. In Acts we see that the secret of the power of the early church was their commitment to:

◆ The Living Lord. (Acts 1:3)
There was no doubt among the believers that Christ was resurrected and that he was alive.

◆ Presence and power of the Holy Spirit. (Acts 1:4-5)
They received God's promised gift—the Holy Spirit.

◆ The second coming of Jesus Christ. (Acts 1:10-11)

These three great truths formed the doctrinal foundation for the early church and are seen many times in the book of Acts. The believers acted as they did because they firmly believed these three truths. They shared a common ideology, a common philosophy about the place of God's people in the development of history. Life was more than existence, more than making a living, more than having an earthly family; it was being a part of God's eternal family.

4. There was a common commission. They had a reason for living, and dying if necessary. Acts 1:8 tells us of that mission in

life. *But when the Holy Spirit comes upon you, you will be filled with power, and you will be witnesses for me in Jerusalem, in all of Judea and Samaria, and to the ends of the earth.*

The sharing of the Living Lord in the power of the Holy Spirit became their reason for living. This was their mission in life. All they did was related to this mission. They met to share. They met to pray. They met to study. They met to fellowship. All of their meetings and organization were related to an effective sharing of the Good News of the Living Lord. The bold proclamation of the Good News was always an outgrowth of times of prayer and fellowship. Organizational structure was developed when necessary to enhance the life of the church. The church was able to spread quickly because the members were busy sharing the faith rather than trying to keep the organizations running smoothly. They were quite unlike one pastor of today who said, "Our church is so well organized that the Holy Spirit could be gone a month before we missed Him." The church of the New Testament was like light in darkness. Wherever members went, they took the light of the Gospel and dispelled the darkness. Into the homes the loving church went; into pagan religions the church went; into courts of kings the church went; to the poor the church went; always changing the hearts of people through the power of the preached Word.

Conclusion
A local church of today is to be nothing less than the New Testament church as described above. A church is a band of believers filled with the Holy Spirit, set out on a mission to lead people from darkness to light. The church penetrates society with personal love as she uses her sword, the powerful and holy Word of God. This church will be victorious. Every church must always give attention to the basics of prayer, fellowship, and feasting on the Word. These are the fountains of life for the church.

Chapter 32

WHAT IS A HEALTHY INDIGENOUS CHURCH?

The word "indigenous" means something native, domestic, national. It is that which springs from and develops within a particular culture. Farming with a carabao is indigenous to the Philippines.

An indigenous church is a church that is basically made up of nationals. It is able to grow within the culture where it finds itself. It is a pattern of church growth under the leadership of the Holy Spirit, that sets people free to be and do all God wants them to be and do. It means freedom from the bondage of dependence on external finances and personnel. (This is not to say that all help from outside the congregation is wrong.)

We will look at five "selfs" in the indigenous church.

When using the word "self" so often in the following few pages we must always remember that without Christ, a person or a church can do nothing worthwhile. Scripture worth always remembering is found in 2 Corinthians 3:4-6a. It says, *We say this because we have confidence in God through Christ. There is nothing in us that allows us to claim that we are capable of doing this work. The capacity we have comes from God. It is he who made us capable of serving the new covenant...*

1. **The indigenous church is self-governing.**

From Colossians 1:17-18 we read: *Christ existed before all things, and in union with him all things have their proper place. He is the head of his body, the church; he is the source of the body's life.*

Self-governing means that the local church is able to make its own decisions under the Lordship of Jesus Christ. The local church should not be under the control of any foreign body. This foreign body may be a fellowship of churches such as an association or convention, or a mission board. The local church may voluntarily cooperate with such groups, but never should a group outside the local church assume authority over the local church. The church should be able to think and act on its own. This can be especially difficult in undeveloped nations when well intentioned missionaries, especially foreigners, bring their ideas and preplanned programs to a church or an association of churches and ask the people to consider adopting the program. As one national said, "How can we say no to an American missionary?" He went on to say, "We may not agree on the proposal, but we are conditioned to say yes." From the beginning, the local church should have the freedom to decide when they will meet, where they will meet, and what they will do when they meet. The local church should, from the birth of the church, be expected to decide who the pastor/leaders will be, how they will be paid, etc. The local church should decide where and when to build their new chapel. The local church should decide if, when, and how they will have evangelistic meetings.

The church may listen to the missionary, whether foreigner or national, but should never allow the outsider to make decisions for the church or put the church in a position where the church cannot say no to suggestions that do not fit its needs.

2. **The indigenous church is self-supporting.**

Read again the Scripture given under the first point, self-governing. It applies here also.

Self-supporting means that the local church takes care of its financial needs through the tithes and offerings of its members. From the beginning of the life of the church, this is possible. It must be remembered that a new church will not have the financial responsibilities of an older church. As the church develops a step at a time, it will grow in its capacity to finance its programs and needs as they develop. Some underdeveloped nations have become so accustomed to dependence on foreign help that for a church to think self-support is revolutionary. With God's help, it is being done by many churches. These churches have a healthy spirit of who they are and what they can do with God's help. Those who simply say, "we cannot," are to be pitied. Those who would say this have never really tried.

Self-support begins very early in the life of a church. Before the church is born, the people provide the meeting place, the lights, and the chairs. After the church is born, members continue to provide the meeting place, song books, Bibles, etc.

The church usually does not need a church building in the beginning. This becomes a long term project of the group. They will secure land and begin to save money. In the beginning a church may not need, nor can it afford, to import a pastor from another place or from a seminary. The church will recognize that God can call and empower members from within the church to lead the worship services and perform the duties of a pastor. The church will pay the expenses for the leaders to attend training seminars and classes that usually will be made available. The church will shoulder all of these training expenses. As the church and leaders develop, one man may be chosen to be the pastor with others helping him. As this pastor gives more and more time to the work of the church, the church will want to begin giving him a set amount of love offering each week. As the church grows, it is possible that they will need a full time pastor and the church will pay him a salary on the level of others in the community.

The self-supporting church has a beautiful dignity and self-esteem.

3. **The indigenous church is self-expressing.**

This means the local church has freedom to choose the days and hours for worship and fellowship. One church may have a very different schedule of meetings from another nearby church. It also means the local church has freedom of expression in worship.

4. **The indigenous church will be self-teaching.**

This means all the members will have a part in teaching one another. It should never be just a pastor or a few select people who teach. Paul said, *My brothers: I myself feel sure that you are full of goodness, that you have all knowledge, and that you are able to teach one another.* Romans 15:14 Also, in 1 Corinthians 14:26,31 Paul speaks of the members teaching one another. To find out how this can be done please study the last chapter of this book that deals with a Bible reading report time.

5. **The indigenous church will be self-propagating.**

In Matthew 28:18-20 Jesus said, *"I have been given all authority in heaven and on earth. Go, then, to all peoples everywhere and make them my disciples: baptize them in the name of the Father, the Son, and the Holy Spirit, and teach them to obey everything I have commanded you. And I will be with you always, to the end of the age."*

Self-propagating means that the church will be involved in starting other new Bible studies that may become churches. It is normal that a church filled with hope and joy will want to spread their new faith with as many people as possible.

Self-governing, self-supporting, self-expressing, and self-teaching come at the very beginning of the life of the new church. Self-propagating does not come as quickly. It takes time for a church to bring about the birth of another church. But from the very beginning there should be the "heart beat" for starting another new church. A member or members may go to a nearby town or community and have a Bible study at the house of a friend or relative. Once there are new believers who are willing to follow the Lord, a new church can be born. A church should not rest until it is involved in spreading the Gospel in such a way that a new church will be born.

In starting a new church, God can use farmers, homemakers, professionals, business men, students, or anyone else who is fully committed to Him. A person does not have to have Bible school or seminary training in order to start a new church. The indigenous church should be able to start another new church in the same way their church was started.

An indigenous church established upon Bible principles and fully yielded to Christ is a vibrant, living, and exciting body of believers, confident and courageous in spreading the Gospel.

Chapter 33

WHO IS THE HEAD OF THE CHURCH?

When a believer thinks of the church, he should think of the New Testament church as seen in the Bible. A New Testament church is one whose origin and teachings are based upon the Bible with Jesus as the head. There is a vast difference between most churches of today and the New Testament church. A major difference is seen as we give the Biblical answer to the question, "Who is the head of the church?"

What does the Bible teach concerning the head of the church?

In Ephesians 1:21-23, Paul says, *Christ did what he had purposed, and made known to us the secret plan he had already decided to complete by means of Christ. This plan, which God will complete when the time is right, is to bring all creation together, everything in heaven and on earth, with Christ as head.*

From Colossians 1:15-18 we read: *Christ is the visible likeness of the invisible God. He is the first-born Son, superior to all created things. For through him God created everything in heaven and on earth, the seen and the unseen things, including spiritual powers, lords, rulers, and authorities. God created the whole universe through him and for him. Christ existed before all things, and in union with him all things have their proper place. He is the head of his body, the church; he is the source of the body's life.*

In Colossians 2:19, the Bible says, *...Christ, who is the head of the body. Under Christ's control the whole body is nourished and held together...*

After reading these verses it is clear beyond question that Christ is the head of the church. He alone is worthy of such a position. No one is worthy to take the place of Jesus as the head of the body, the church. To say that a mere man is the head of the church is idolatry and far from Christian teachings. When anyone other than Christ is recognized as the head of a church, it is not a New Testament church. The pastor is not to be the boss of the local church. He, too, is a servant under the Lordship of Christ.

Christ is the originator, the head, and the sustainer of the church.

Chapter 34

HOW DOES A CHURCH CONDUCT A BUSINESS MEETING?

Every church needs a regularly scheduled time to take care of matters that are not best mixed with the worship services. This would be a time for discussion and decisions on church matters. While this is not the most exciting part of church life, it is necessary for a healthy church. This is usually called a business meeting.

When should the church hold business meetings?

Business meetings should be held on a regular basis. Many churches have a business meeting once a month. The first week of the month is a good time. The meetings can be held on a weekday night or following a Sunday worship service.

Who should lead the church business meeting?

Usually the pastor or church leader will lead or moderate the meeting. If there is no pastor, the church may choose someone to lead the meeting.

The leader must be an active, respected church member. The leader guides the church as they discuss and make decisions on church matters.

What is the atmosphere of the church business meeting?

The church should enter this time in a serious and prayerful mood. It is a time when the life and the activities of the church will be discussed.

Who may attend the church business meeting?

Normally only the church members should attend this meeting. It is not for unbelievers or people who are not members. If non-members are present, they should not participate and cannot make motions or vote.

If the business meeting is held following the regular worship service or Bible study, the service should be dismissed as usual. There should be a break to allow members to greet visitors and give visitors the opportunity to leave before the business session begins.

What is a quorum?

A quorum is the number of members that must be present before the church can have an official business meeting. The church should decide the number for the quorum. It should be at least fifty percent of the active members.

Who should keep records of a church business meeting?

The church secretary should keep detailed records of all the decisions made at the business meeting. The church will provide a permanent record book for the secretary.

It is suggested that the secretary record the decisions in a temporary notebook. At the next business meeting the secretary's report will be read from the temporary notebook. After the report has been approved by the church, it will be recorded in the permanent record book.

What is the church to do if there is an emergency?

A special business meeting can be called to take care of emergency matters. These are matters that cannot wait until the regular monthly business meeting. A quorum is required at emergency business meetings also. If possible, all members should be informed ahead of time about the emergency meeting.

This order may be followed in the business meeting.

1. Devotional - This is a Scripture reading with brief comments, then prayer asking God's leadership during the meeting. (If business meeting follows the worship service, a Scripture reading may not be desired.)

2. Reading of the minutes - The secretary reads from the temporary record book the proceedings of the last business meeting.

The moderator will say, "You have heard the reading of the minutes. Are there any corrections or additions? If there are none the minutes will stand approved as read." If there are corrections, the minutes will be approved as corrected.

3. Treasurer's report - The church treasurer, if possible, will write the report on a blackboard so all can see. (Some churches will have copies to distribute to the members.) The report will be as follows:

(1) The ending balance of the previous month.
(2) The amount of each week's offerings.
(3) The total of offerings for the month.
(4) All expenditures itemized and briefly explained.
(5) The current balance after expenditures have been subtracted.

The moderator will say, "Are there any corrections or additions to the reading of the treasurer's report? Do you have any questions?"

Time will be given for questions. Then the moderator will say, "Do I hear a motion that the treasurer's report be accepted?"

Someone will make a motion such as, "I move the report be accepted." Another will say, "I second the motion." The moderator then will say, "All those favoring the acceptance of the treasurer's report raise your hand. Any opposed, raise your hand."

4. Report from leaders of Bible studies.

5. Report of the Sunday School.

6. Any other reports.

7. Unfinished business. These are items that have been talked about in previous business meetings and need more discussion.

8. New Business.

This is the time to bring before the church any changes—new teachers, new officers, new organizations, proposed purchases, problems, recommendations, receiving new members, etc. Everything that happens in the life of the church is the business of the church.

9. Adjournment.

After the business has been discussed, someone will make a motion that the meeting be adjourned (ended). This will be seconded and voted by the church.

10. Closing prayer.

It is well to remember that the business meeting is a time when every church member can be open and honest with each other. It is not a place for heated debate or arguments. All that is done should be done with the awareness that the Holy Spirit is in control of the life of the church, and that Christ is to be honored in everything.

Chapter 35

WHAT ARE THE QUALIFICATIONS AND RESPONSIBILITIES OF A CHURCH TREASURER?

After the birth of a new church, one of the first church officers elected is the treasurer. This is necessary because one part of the worship service is the giving of tithes and offerings. Someone must be officially responsible for the correct recording of the amount of the offerings and for the security of the money.

QUALIFICATIONS OF THE CHURCH TREASURER

From 1 Timothy 3:8-13 we read Paul's list of qualifications for workers in the church, which would include a church treasurer. *Church helpers must also have a good character and be sincere; they must not drink too much wine or be greedy for money; they should hold to the revealed truth of the faith with a clear conscience. They should be tested first, and then, if they pass the test, they are to serve. Their wives also must be of good character and must not gossip; they must be sober and honest in everything. A church helper must have only one wife, and be able to manage his children and family well. Those helpers who do their work well win for themselves a good standing and are able to speak boldly about their faith in Christ Jesus.*

Look briefly at the list.
1. Must have a good character and be sincere.
2. Must not drink too much wine. Many medical experts and alcoholics anonymous members would say that any alcoholic beverage is too much.
3. Must not be greedy for money. The Bible says that the love of money is the root of all evil. (1 Timothy 6:10)

4. Must hold to the revealed truth found in the Bible.
5. Must be mature.
6. The wife or husband must not be a gossip.
7. Must be sober and honest in everything.
8. Must have only one wife.
9. Must be able to manage his family.
10. Must share his faith boldly.

Some of the above qualifications may be stated in another way.

The treasurer must be:
1. Born again.
2. A faithful and active member of the local church. No one should be considered for this position until they have officially been received for membership by the church.
3. Very regular in church attendance. A person cannot do the job if he is not there.
4. Completely honest.
5. Able to keep clear records.
6. Should not be a gossip. What people give is between them and God and should be confidential.
7. Willing to give monthly financial reports to the church.

RESPONSIBILITIES OF THE TREASURER

1. Count the amount of the tithes and offerings after each worship service. The assistant treasurer should always be present and confirm the total.

2. After the treasurer and assistant treasurer have counted the offering, the amount is to be recorded in the treasurer's book. The assistant treasurer should sign or initial the amount entered. When working with money, church members cannot be too careful. They must remain above suspicion. Using safety measures does not mean that a person is dishonest. It does help to remove any possible temptation or any suspicion by other members.

3. The treasurer and assistant treasurer should open a savings or checking account at a bank designated by the church.

4. Deposits should be made each week. It is not wise to leave money at the house of the treasurer.

5. The treasurer or assistant treasurer are not allowed to make any expenditure unless authorized by the church. Authorization can be given at a regular business meeting or at an emergency business meeting.

6. The treasurer or assistant are strictly forbidden to make loans from the church funds to anyone—even to church members, not even in cases of emergency.

7. At the regular monthly business meeting of the church, the treasurer will give a financial report. The treasurer will begin by reporting the balance at the beginning of the month. Then the report will show the amounts received each week. The individual expenditures of the month will then be reported. The report will end with the balance remaining in the bank and in petty cash. The treasurer's records should be open for all church members to see. The treasurer should not be afraid of questions from members concerning the finances of the church.

QUALIFICATIONS OF THE ASSISTANT should be the same as for the treasurer.

These officers should be elected by the church at the annual election of all officers, teachers, etc. (Many churches have these elections at the beginning of January.) The treasurer and the assistant may be re-elected if they are doing their jobs well. If they fail to meet the basic qualifications or fail to fulfill their responsibilities, they should be replaced. This replacement can be done in the middle of the year or at the regular annual elections.

Chapter 36

WHAT ARE THE QUALIFICATIONS AND RESPONSIBILITIES OF A CHURCH SECRETARY?

QUALIFICATIONS OF THE CHURCH SECRETARY

The same basic qualifications of the church treasurer would apply to the secretary (sometimes called clerk). Please refer to qualifications for church treasurer or read 1 Timothy 3:8-13.

1. The church secretary must be an active member of the local church.

2. The secretary must be elected by the church. This can be done at the annual election of teachers and officers, or at any time the position should become vacant.

3. The secretary must be able to attend the business meetings of the church.

4. The secretary should be able to take notes of what happens in the church life and in the business sessions. The writing should be neat, clear, and easy to understand.

RESPONSIBILITIES OF THE CHURCH SECRETARY

1. When the church has the regular monthly business meeting the secretary is to keep a record of all items voted on. Each motion is to be recorded and then stated if it was accepted or rejected.

2. At each business meeting the secretary is to read the records (called minutes) of the last business meeting.

3. The secretary is to maintain a good and up-to-date record of the membership roll of the church.

4. The secretary adds or removes names on the membership roll only with the approval of the church.

5. The secretary safeguards the record books.

6. As detailed and complete records are recorded from month to month and year to year, the secretary is compiling a history of the church.

Chapter 37

WHAT ARE THE QUALIFICATIONS FOR A PASTOR?

We find a list of many of the qualifications for church leaders in 1 Timothy 3:1-7:

This is a true saying: If a man is eager to be a church leader, he desires an excellent work. A church leader must be without fault; he must have only one wife, be sober, self-controlled, and orderly; he must welcome strangers in his home; he must be able to teach; he must not be a drunkard or a violent man, but gentle and peaceful; he must not love money; he must be able to manage his own family well and make his children obey him with all respect. For if a man does not know how to manage his own family, how can he take care of the church of God? He must be mature in the faith, so that he will not swell up with pride and be condemned, as the Devil was. He should be a man who is respected by the people outside the church, so that he will not be disgraced and fall into the Devil's trap.

QUALIFICATIONS FOR A PASTOR

1. He must be born again.

2. He must know without a doubt that God has called him to do the work of a pastor. In the Bible we see many examples of men called by God.

Moses - *I am sending you to the king of Egypt so that you can lead my people out of his country.* Exodus 3:10

Samuel - *The Lord came and stood there, and called as he had before, "Samuel, Samuel!" Samuel answered, "Speak; your servant is listening."* 1 Samuel 3:10

Amos - *But the Lord took me from my work as a shepherd and ordered me to go and prophesy to his people Israel.* Amos 7:15

Isaiah - *Then I heard the Lord say, "Whom shall I send? Who will be our messenger?" I answered, "I will go! Send me!"* Isaiah 6:8

Jeremiah - *The Lord said to me, "I chose you before I gave you life, and before you were born I selected you to be a prophet to the nations." I answered, "Sovereign Lord, I don't know how to speak; I am too young." But the Lord said to me, "Do not say that you are too young, but go to the people I send you to, and tell them everything I command you to say. Do not be afraid of them, for I will be with you to protect you. I, the Lord, have spoken!"* Jeremiah 1:4-8

Ezekiel - *"Mortal man, I am sending you to the people of Israel. ...They are stubborn and do not respect me, so I am sending you to tell them what I, the Sovereign Lord, am saying to them. Whether those rebels listen to you or not, they will know that a prophet has been among them."* Ezekiel 2:3-5

Paul - *The Lord said, "Go, because I have chosen him to serve me. to make my name known to Gentiles and kings and to the people of Israel."* Acts 9:15 Also in Galatians 1:15 Paul says, *But God in his grace chose me even before I was born, and called me to serve him.*

3. The effective pastor must be committed—committed to preach the Gospel, to care for the flock.

4. If he is to be used in a great way, he must be a man of prayer.

5. The effective pastor must be a student of the Word of God. He must learn well what the Bible says. From 2 Timothy 2:15 we read: *Do your best to win full approval in God's sight, as a worker who is not ashamed of his work, one who correctly teaches the message of God's truth.*

6. From the Scriptures given earlier in the lesson, we see a number of other qualifications for a pastor.

   (1) He must have only one wife.
   (2) He must be sober, self-controlled, and orderly.
   (3) He must welcome strangers into his house. He must love people.
   (4) He must be able to teach.
   (5) He must not be a drunkard, violent, but gentle and peaceful.
   (6) He must not love money. (This does not say he must be poor and without necessary finances.)
   (7) He must be able to manage his own family and have the respect of his children.
   (8) He must be mature in faith. (This does not say that the pastor must be an old man.)
   (9) He should be respected by the people outside the church.

What about a pastor for a new church?

The church should have worship services and Bible study immediately after the birth of the church. Should the church go outside the group to get a more mature pastor? It depends on the strength of the church. Is a full time pastor needed? How much money does the church receive weekly from the members to be used to pay a pastor's salary? Most new churches are not ready for and cannot afford a seminary trained "professional" pastor.

This may sometimes be a blessing, because it forces the members to take leadership responsibilities and grow as they become involved. Of course, there should be leadership training made available for the new leaders. A pastor/leader must be prepared. For some, part of this preparation may come from formal studies at a Bible school or seminary. Others will have to get their training in the same way Paul did. From the second chapter of Galatians we read about Paul's credentials and qualifications as a preacher of the Gospel. (A person who does not get formal classroom training should not feel inferior to those who do.)

It is God, His call, His guidance, His power, His Word that makes a man a great preacher of the gospel.

It is not necessary to call a pastor in the beginning. Church members who meet most of the above qualifications can share leadership responsibilities. Three or four men may rotate in leading the worship service each Sunday. They are not called pastors or thought of as pastors. After a year or so of study concerning the work of the pastor, it is likely that one or two of them will feel God's call to continue the work of a pastor. This feeling will be shared by the congregation. The members will have an impression from the Holy Spirit about who has been given the gift of pastoring.

Chapter 38

HOW DOES A CHURCH GET A PASTOR?

Several factors influence a church getting a pastor.

The size of the congregation.
The needs of the congregation.
The financial strength of the congregation.
The age of the church.
The availability of pastoral leadership outside the congregation.

It is wrong to assume that a church must get a pastor from outside the congregation. God can, and often does, call men from the membership of the church to serve as pastors/leaders. At all times the Holy Spirit should guide the church in the matter of calling a man to be their pastor.

We will look at two common situations when churches need to get pastors.

How does the new church with a small membership and limited financial resources get a pastor?

The new church may ask one or more of the members to alternate leading the worship services. These men will preach/teach/lead. There will be a need for weekly leadership training classes for those chosen. These classes will be very basic, dealing with the very practical aspects of pastoral work. Emphasis will be put on how to prepare a sermon and how to do other pastoral duties. It needs to be pointed out that the traditional style of worship is not always needed nor even best, especially when a church is young with leaders of little experience. A song service led by a member, followed with the reading and discussion of a chapter from the

Bible, may be just as effective as the traditional three songs and a sermon. Both may be effective.

Wide participation by the members is very desirable. The same person should not lead the singing, play the guitar, pray, teach, and preach.

Normally at this early stage, the worship leader should not be thought of as the pastor. It may be a while before the leaders and church members are sure who has been given the gift of pastoring. But in time all will know. If five men start out rotating as worship leaders, after a few months this number may be down to two men. Both of these may end up being regular leaders. It will usually be best for one to be recognized as pastor and the other as associate pastor. There is strength in having two or more leaders sharing the preaching, especially if they are bivocational. (By bivocational we mean that they may continue to make their living by teaching, farming, or some other way, and at the same time serve the church.) The burden is lighter when two or more share in the responsibilities. Preparing one or two new sermons every week can become too heavy for a new Christian with little training and he may become discouraged under the work load.

The position of pastor/leader is often settled within a year after the birth of the church. Even though these men may be making a living with their regular work, the church should begin as soon as possible giving a weekly love gift to the pastor/leader. As the church grows, the amount of this love gift should also grow. Any church related expenses, such as attending learning seminars, special classes, study materials, and travel expenses, should be paid by the church.

These men are no less pastors than highly trained men serving full time in large churches.

As the church grows in number and is financially able to pay a full salary, it may be best to think of looking for a full time pastor. It is possible that the person serving on a part time basis may quit his outside work and begin serving as full time pastor. Through personal study, the bivocational pastor may become as well trained as a man who has completed Bible school or seminary training. But the church may desire to look for a pastor from outside the local church who has more training.

How does the larger, financially able church find a pastor?

1. After much prayer, the congregation comes to a common agreement that a full time pastor is needed and that, through the tithes and offering of the members, a full time salary can be paid.

2. The congregation will elect a search committee of three to five members to begin looking for a pastor. This committee will be open to suggestions from members about the kind of pastor they want.

3. There are several places a search committee may begin looking for a new pastor. They may look for Bible school graduates, seminary graduates, or pastors of other churches.

The committee may get information about prospective pastors by talking to professors, fellow students, and by talking to church members and leaders who know them.

4. Some things the committee will want to know about a prospective pastor:

Does he have a clear conversion experience?
Does he have a clear call of God to preach?
Does he have a burning desire to preach?
Does he believe the Bible to be the Word of God?
Does he preach the Word with authority?

Is he a "soul-winner?"
Does he witness regularly?
Is his moral reputation good?
Is he a hard worker?
Does he tithe?
Does he pay his debts?

The committee will need to talk to a number of people and to the preacher in order to get all this information. (Chapter 36, "What are the qualifications for a pastor?" may be helpful at this point.)

5. The committee should hear him preach at least one time. If the committee is favorably impressed, he could be invited to preach at their church.

If the preacher is married, it is important that his family attend the services when he preaches. It is best if arrangements can be made for him to preach two times on Sunday. A special time of fellowship, such as a noon meal on Sunday where all the members attend, can be helpful in getting to know the guest preacher.

6. The committee may desire to have a brief meeting with the prospective pastor to discuss such things as doctrine, salary, allowances, expectations, responsibilities, etc.

7. A special meeting may be scheduled on the following Sunday for the church to share their feelings about the prospective pastor. The search committee may share their findings and present a recommendation. The church will vote on whether to invite him. Voting is often done by secret balloting with each member simply writing a "yes" or "no" on a paper. (Secret balloting usually will give members the opportunity to vote according to the way they really feel instead of the way they think they are expected to vote.)

It is desirable that the vote be near unanimous. It would seem unwise for a pastor to accept an invitation if the vote was only 51% yes and 49% no. The church may decide that two-thirds or more must be yes before extending an invitation. The church faces a great responsibility when asking a man to lead them. Much prayer and study must precede the search for the right man and the calling of the man to be the pastor.

Chapter 39

SHOULD OUR PASTOR BE ORDAINED?

First, we need to understand the meaning of "ordain." The dictionary gives several definitions.

1. To order, to decree.
2. To appoint authoritatively.
3. To destine or predestine.
4. To invest with ministerial functions.

Various religious groups have their own ideas about the importance and way of ordination.

What is the Biblical view of being ordained?

All great men of God in the Bible had a sense of being ordained of God to do certain things, to preach a certain message, to go to a certain place. It was this sense of being ordained (ordered, chosen) that motivated these men to risk their lives for the One who commissioned them.

Biblical ordination is basically, and most importantly, a special relationship between God and a person, wherein God gives that person a sacred responsibility. The responsibility normally is to share a message of judgment, hope, and freedom through faith in God.

Note some examples of men ordained by God for a special task.

Moses
The Israelites were in Egyptian bondage. God said to Moses, *Now I am sending you to the king of Egypt so that you can lead my people out of his country.* Exodus 3:10

Moses was ordained in the most meaningful way. God called him personally. Moses went and a nation was rescued from bondage.

Jeremiah

The prophet Jeremiah lived during the last part of the seventh century and the first part of the sixth century B.C. Israel was living in sin and rebellion against God. From the Bible we read of how God ordained Jeremiah to warn the nation of coming doom:

The Lord said to me, "I chose you before I gave you life, and before you were born I selected you to be a prophet to the nations." I answered, "Sovereign Lord, I don't know how to speak; I am too young." But the Lord said to me, "Do not say that you are too young, but go to the people I send you to, and tell them everything I command you to say." Jeremiah 1:4-7

Jeremiah was commissioned, chosen, ordered, ordained. He went and spoke the message God ordered him to speak. This is ordination.

Ezekiel

This prophet lived in exile in Babylon during the period before and after the fall of Jerusalem in 586 B.C. His was a message of warning, repentance, and hope. It all began when he was commissioned by God.

This was the dazzling light which shows the presence of the Lord. When I saw this, I fell face downward on the ground. Then I heard a voice saying, "Mortal man, stand up. I want to talk to you." While the voice was speaking, God's spirit entered me and raised me to my feet, and I heard the voice continue, "Mortal man, I am sending you to the people of Israel...I am sending you to tell them what I, the Sovereign Lord, am saying to them." Ezekiel 1:28-2:3,5

Ezekiel was ordained by God to go to a certain people with a special message. He went and God blessed him.

Paul
In the New Testament days there was a man who was fighting against Christianity. This man Paul had a conversion experience that changed all his life. Only a few days after Paul's conversion God sent Ananias to minister to him. *The Lord said to him, "Go, because I have chosen him to serve me, to make my name known to Gentiles and kings and to the people of Israel."* Acts 9:15

Paul was ordained, ordered, commissioned by God, and this was sufficient for him to begin preaching immediately after his conversion experience. *He stood up and was baptized; and after he had eaten, his strength came back. Saul stayed for a few days with the believers in Damascus. He went straight to the synagogues and began to preach that Jesus was the Son of God. All who heard him were amazed and asked, "Isn't he the one who in Jerusalem was killing those who worship that man Jesus? And didn't he come here for the very purpose of arresting those people and taking them back to the chief priests?" But Saul's preaching became even more powerful...* Acts 9:18-22

Concerning his call, Paul said, *From Paul, whose call to be an apostle did not come from man or by means of man, but from Jesus Christ and God the Father, who raised Him from death.* Galatians 1:1

Paul was ordained, chosen, commissioned by God. Based on this ordination he preached powerfully.

There are many other illustrations in the Old and New Testaments of men called by God. These men found adequate motivation in that call to go forth and do as God told them to do.

You will note that in the lives of these men, the necessary ordination came from God, not from men. All of these men recognized that they had been ordained by God for a special ministry. They did not have man's approval or orders before launching into their ministry.

What does the New Testament say about ordination?

John 15:16 - *You did not choose me; I chose you and appointed you to go and bear much fruit.* The word "appointed" may mean ordained.

Acts 14:23 - *In each church they appointed elders, and with prayers and fasting they commended them to the Lord, in whom they had put their trust.* The word, "appoint" which can be translated "ordained," is used when certain elders were chosen by Paul and Barnabas on their return visit to the churches during their first missionary journey. The Greek word used here means, "to elect by stretching out the hand."

There is no formal description of an ordination service in the New Testament. There was the custom of recognizing those who had been called by God. So the formal service may be thought of more as a recognition of ordination. The church or churches are recognizing publicly that they believe a man has been ordained by God for a special ministry. They are confirming what they believe has already happened.

A church's responsibility in the recognition service.

1. The church should have time to observe a man to see that he is a godly man possessing the gift of pastoring/preaching. The church should examine closely the Bible qualifications of a church leader found in 1 Timothy 3:1-7 and Titus.

2. The church will initiate the scheduling of the recognition service.

3. The church may invite sister churches to participate in the recognition service.

The Recognition Service

This is a special and sacred time filled with both solemnness and joy. The order of the service may be as follows:

1. Welcome, opening remarks, and prayer.

2. Appropriate music.

3. Introduction of the preacher who has been ordained.

4. A time for a council or committee to question the preacher. These questions may include: when he was born again, when he was called to preach, what is his view of the Bible as the inspired Word of God, and various doctrines.

5. The council may have a few minutes to privately discuss their impressions. They will then come to a conclusion. They may decide to: a. recognize as ordained, b. not recognize as ordained, c. defer judgment until a later time.

6. The council presents their recommendation to the church.

7. A respected man of God will preach a sermon which will include a challenge and charge to the preacher.

8. Prayer of thanksgiving and asking God's blessing.

9. The practice as seen in 1 Timothy 4:14 may be followed when each of the ordaining council will pass by the kneeling preacher and place their hands on his head.

10. Presentation of preacher with full recognition of ordination.

11. Closing prayer.

Some churches give the preacher a good quality Bible.

Questions some people ask:

Can a preacher be effective without this formal recognition service? Yes, without a doubt.

Must a person have this formal recognition service before he can preach? Of course not; look at Paul.

Can a preacher or pastor perform a baptismal service without having a formal recognition service? Yes, he may. The Bible does not prohibit it.

Can a pastor lead in the Lord's Supper if he has not had a formal ordination service? Yes.

Is there a set way in which the recognition service must be done? No, there is not. There is little in the Bible about a ritualistic ordination service.

Can a man be a full time pastor without having had a public ordination service? Yes.

How old must a man be before he can be recognized as having been ordained of God? Any age at which he gives evidence of having been ordained of God.

Conclusion:

It is well to remember that a man's call must come from God. His power must come from God. His message must come from God. His authority must come from God. Men may or may not put their stamp of approval on a man who has been called by God. Those who have not had the blessing of a recognition service should not be thought of as inferior or less of a pastor or preacher than those who have had a recognition service. It is sad to see how some religious groups put a man on a pious ecclesiastical pedestal by giving him a special title such as "reverend" if he has been ordained by man. This is a class system promoting pride and is definitely not Biblical.

A recognition service can be a very beautiful and meaningful event in the life of the preacher and in the life of the church. It seems wise that, after a due time of ministry and testing, a man should receive a public recognition by a church (preferably the church he is serving). This recognition is a time when the church can proudly join hands publicly with the preacher and say, "We are with you, and believe God has called you for a special ministry."

Chapter 40

SHOULD A PASTOR HAVE AN OUTSIDE JOB?

Should a pastor do the work of the pastor and also have income from another job? The answer to this question depends upon the financial needs of the pastor's family, as well as the ability of the church to pay a full salary.

Churches with a small membership often cannot pay a pastor an adequate salary. In cases such as this, it is right that the pastor work, either full time or part time, in order to meet the financial needs of his family. Men who do this are called "bivocational pastors." A large percentage of churches around the world are pastored by men who have outside work. The pastor who is too good to do secular work when the need arises is not good enough to be a pastor. There is dignity in work, even in manual labor. There is little dignity in the man who says, "God has called me to preach, therefore, it is wrong for me to do any other kind of work." If a pastor does not receive enough money to support his family, he is not to sit and wait for a miracle or beg; he is to search for any kind of honorable work, even on a temporary basis. Paul was speaking to leaders when he said, *But if anyone does not take care of his relatives, especially the members of his own family, he has denied the faith and is worse than an unbeliever.* 1 Timothy 5:8

Paul is an outstanding example of one who was a great preacher of the gospel, yet sometimes did other kinds of work to make a living. In Acts 18:1-4 the Bible says, *After this, Paul left Athens and went on to Corinth. There he met a Jew named Aquila, born in Pontus, who had recently come from Italy with his wife Priscilla, for Emperor Claudius had ordered all the Jews to leave Rome. Paul went to see them, and stayed and worked with them, because he earned his living by making tents, just as they did. He held discussions in the synagogue every Sabbath, trying to convince both Jews and Greeks.*

Conclusions:

It is healthy for a man to desire to give as much time as possible to the preaching of the Gospel. The desire to be a full-time pastor is normal.

It is unhealthy for a man to fail to meet the physical needs of his family. A man has no message to preach if he is not properly caring for his family. If the church the pastor is serving cannot pay an adequate salary, he should seek part time or full time work. The work of the pastor outside the church can be blessed by God, even as his work in the church can be blessed by God.

Chapter 41

HOW DO I PREPARE A SERMON?

1. From the beginning of the preparation of a sermon to the end of the preached sermon, all you do must be saturated with serious prayer.

2. You must be aware that preaching a sermon is a very serious task. It is not entertainment.

3. You must be trying to live for God every day. You must be a good example.

4. You must be a student of the Bible. This does not mean that you must know all that is in the Bible, but that you are always studying it to learn all you can. (This does not mean that you must have formal training in Bible school or seminary.)

5. You must be a student of human behavior.

6. You must recognize the source of your knowledge and strength. It is the Holy Spirit who guides and empowers.

TIME TO PREPARE

Know who the target is. Know who you are going to preach to. There are two broad categories, the unsaved and the saved.

Unsaved
If the target is unsaved people, the message will need to be evangelistic. It should tell people why they need to be saved and how they can be saved. The Bible is filled with passages that apply to

the unsaved. Some of these are: Acts 16; Acts 2; Romans 3-5,10; John 1,3,5; Ephesians 2; Galatians 2; Mark 8,10.

Saved

This target is those who have been born again. Usually in the regular worship service, most of those who attend have been born again. But within this target there are many needs to be met which will demand different kinds of sermons.

This means that the more the preacher knows about the spiritual condition of the people, the better he can hit the target. By "hitting the target," we mean preaching a sermon that will meet the needs of the people. Among the general target—believers, the preacher needs to try to be sensitive to the greatest needs of the group. (Do not determine the greatest need of one person and preach to that person.)

Among the believers the preacher may see certain needs that should be met. Some of these needs may be:

◆ ENCOURAGEMENT to remain faithful.

The Bible is full of passages for this kind of sermon. Some good examples are: Hebrews 11,12; Galatians 5; Colossians 3; Philippians 3; Joshua 1; Jonah 1-4.

◆ REDEDICATION for those who have grown cold spiritually. (Encouragement to repent and return.)

Some examples of good passages to use are: Psalm 51; Luke 15; Romans 12; Psalms 32,139.

◆ COMFORT in times of sorrow.

Passages which may meet such needs are: Psalm 23; John 14; John 10; 2 Corinthians 4.

◆ INDOCTRINATION. People are always in need of a greater knowledge of the great teachings of the Bible. These teachings are called doctrines and can be found in nearly every chapter in the Bible. Some great doctrinal passages are:

Love - 2 Corinthians 13; **Sin** - Romans 3,6,7; **Death** - 1 Corinthians 15, 2 Corinthians 4,5; **Second Coming of Christ** - 1 Thessalonians 4, Acts 1; **Baptism** - Acts 8, Matthew 3; **Cross of Christ** - Luke 23, 1 Corinthians 2; **Security of the believer** - Romans 8.

◆ INSPIRATION. People are always in need of inspiration for living the Christian life. Philippians 1-4; 1 Thessalonians 5; Romans 5; Acts 2,3,4; Nehemiah 6; Joshua 24; Matthew 28:18-20; Matthew 5-7

Through fellowship with the people, a preacher can know some of the greatest needs of a group. From this knowledge of where the people are in their spiritual pilgrimage, the preacher can ask God for the message that best meets the needs of the group. The greater his Bible knowledge and prayer, the more likely the preacher will find the Bible message for the hour.

In review we see that:

1. The preacher must be personally prepared to preach. This means personal commitment to Christ, a clean life, being a student of the Bible, and being a man of prayer.

2. He must recognize the target (those who will be hearing).

3. He must zero in on the target, determining specific needs which should be met through the preaching of the message.

4. He must prayerfully seek God's message from the Bible which will meet the needs of the hearers.

HOW TO PREPARE THE MESSAGE

Much of the preparation has been done when the first four steps have been taken. But there is more preparation.

The passage of Scripture must be found in which God speaks to the needs of people. (There is nothing better than for a preacher to read the Bible daily, at least 20 chapters a week and if he has time he will want to read more. Reading the entire Bible at least once every year will do more for a preacher than any kind of special training. When he knows the Bible he will know where to look for Scriptures to meet needs.)

Once you have found the text—the Scripture you will use as a basis for the sermon—you will want to read and reread it. Analyze it word by word and verse by verse. Take notes. Find key words. Try to outline the passage. Find the major truths in the text. Find passages in other parts of the Bible that teach the same lesson and use the verses in your sermon. Use stories in the Bible to illustrate the great truths you have found in the text.

Prayerfully study the passage, always asking God for wisdom and power. Then when the hour comes for you to preach, your heart will be bubbling over with excitement about God's message which you must deliver to the people.

There are fine points about preaching that a person will want to study, but when the above things are done, a man can preach a very powerful and relevant sermon. Lives will be changed when God's Word is preached. Remember the key to success is **a committed man** under the **rule of the Holy Spirit** preaching **God's Word**.

Chapter 42

HOW DO I GIVE AN INVITATION?

A sermon is usually followed with an invitation. An invitation is a time when the hearers have an opportunity to respond to the message that has been preached. Always the preacher should expect some response to the message. This response may not always mean a public decision after the sermon. Deep, silent responses are sometimes made without a public invitation being given. But most of the time there are people in the audience who need to make public decisions. This means that usually the preacher needs to give an invitation for these people to openly acknowledge their decisions.

Why do some pastors not give public invitations?

1. They do not have an urgent message that calls for response.

2. They do not have an awareness of the lost condition of man.

3. They are timid, not having the boldness that comes from God, a boldness that should characterize every preacher.

4. They are untrained in how to give an invitation.

Imagine a man with a truck full of food. He gathers a crowd of people who are starving and declares to them that he has plenty of food. He describes the food in detail; the people are licking their lips in anticipation. The man tells the people that it is free to all. He tells them in detail what they must do in order to get the food. Then as the multitude waits, the man gets into his truck and drives off. He never did say, come and eat.

This is the picture of a man who preaches about the way of eternal life and never says to the people, "Come." The "come" is the invitation. It was a cruel thing the man did with the food. It is more cruel for the preacher to describe the new life of peace, joy, and purpose and then not give a clear invitation to the people to accept, to decide to follow Christ.

God gives the preacher the message so that people can be called, invited to follow.

Without apology, Jesus publicly called men to follow Him. *After John had been put in prison, Jesus went to Galilee and preached the Good News from God. "The right time has come," he said, "and the Kingdom of God is near! Turn away from your sins and believe the Good News!" As Jesus walked along the shore of Lake Galilee, he saw two fishermen, Simon and his brother Andrew, catching fish with a net. Jesus said to them, "Come with me, and I will teach you to catch men." At once they left their nets and went with him.* Mark 1:14-18

Jesus went further down the road and saw James and John. *As soon as Jesus saw them, he called them; they left their father Zebedee in the boat with the hired men and went with Jesus.* Mark 1:20

We read that on another occasion, *Jesus went back again to the shore of Lake Galilee. A crowd came to him, and he started teaching them. As he walked along, he saw a tax collector, Levi son of Alphaeus, sitting in his office. Jesus said to him, "Follow me." Levi got up and followed him.* Mark 2:13-14

You will note that Jesus preached the good news of the Kingdom of God, then He invited men to make a decision to follow Him. Also you will note that there was a crowd, yet Jesus was not ashamed to call these men from the crowd. He did not apologize. His call was straightforward; it was clear; it was made directly to the people. The decisions were made publicly. The crowd, the friends, and family members heard the message also, but only a few stepped out publicly to follow. Concerning a public decision, Jesus said, *"If anyone declares publicly that he belongs to me, I will do the same for him before my Father in heaven. But if anyone rejects me publicly, I will reject him before my Father in heaven."* Matthew 10:32-33

As you study the Gospels, you will find that Jesus preached messages directly to the hearts of people, then He called for them to make a decision. He gave an invitation for people to respond.

How is the preacher to give an invitation?

1. First, he must decide to give a clear and meaningful invitation after each message he preaches.

2. He must know that the invitation is part of the sermon.

He should not finish the sermon and add on the invitation. The invitation is the closing part of the sermon. This means that the topic of the sermon will determine what kind of invitation is to be given. If he preaches on tithing, the invitation will be for people to decide to tithe. If he preaches on prayer, the invitation may be for Christians to give more time to prayer. If he preaches to a group of very faithful church members, it is not likely that he will give an invitation for them to come forward to be born again. The invitation may be for greater commitment to Christ.

3. Because the invitation is a part of the sermon, when he prepares it, he will also prepare the last part of the sermon—the invitation.

4. It is usually appropriate to have singing as part of the invitation time.

The invitation song is a part of the sermon. The preacher should prayerfully choose which song will be used. The choice of the song should normally be done in consultation with the one in charge of music. This decision should be made before the worship service begins. The song should be well known by those who are to sing. The entire congregation will often sing the invitation song. Sometimes only a choir will sing.

5. The preacher must make a detailed explanation of what he wants the people to do—the invitation must be clear.

It is not enough for him to say, "Come to the front if you want to follow Jesus." He needs to explain why they should come to the front. He should tell them what they are going to do when they get there. Unsaved people are fearful and apprehensive. They may think they will be baptized on that day if they come seeking Christ.

6. The preacher should not trick people into making decisions.

If the preacher asks people to raise their hands to indicate that they need to be saved, he should not then ask everyone who raised their hands to come to the front. This is tricking people.

7. The invitation should be personal.

The preacher should not look out the window while giving an invitation. He should not gaze at the notes on the pulpit or at the hymn book. He should look deep into the hearts of the people as he sees their faces, their eyes, their expressions. (This is not to suggest staring into the eyes of one person for a long time.) In making the invitation personal, the preacher should use personal pronouns such as you, your family, your life, our, we, I, etc.

8. The preacher should have continuity between his closing words of the message and the singing of the invitation song.

The preacher moves smoothly and quickly into the introduction of the song and the singing. The song leader should be alert and ready to begin the singing. The pastor should step to the area where he expects people to come when they make their decision. He should not be sidetracked by leading the singing or playing a piano or guitar. When people come forward making their decisions, they need a warm hand shake of welcome and encouragement. A preacher holding a guitar or song book cannot easily do this. He gives an impression of not being available to those who come forward. This may discourage those who want to come but are fearful. The preacher should stand, prayerfully waiting, with only a Bible in his hand.

9. The preacher greets those who come forward and asks them individually what their decisions are. He then will ask them to continue standing facing the front as others come.

When it is clear that no others will respond to the invitation, the preacher will introduce those making decisions and tell why each one has come forward. He then will ask them to be seated at the front and state that he will have a brief time with them following the closing prayer. He thanks the congregation for coming and makes closing remarks. The worship service is closed with prayer.

10. Only qualified people should counsel those making decisions.

This should be someone who can very clearly explain the way of salvation. It should be someone spiritually mature and full of Bible knowledge. Often the preacher will be the one to do the counseling, but this is not always necessary. There should be members trained to do this.

11. If possible, those coming forward should be taken to a private room for counseling. Each one should have personal counseling.

The time of counseling is extremely important. The fact that people come to the front seeking salvation does not mean that they have found salvation. Seeking and finding are different. To raise a hand indicating that they are not saved but are interested is not the same as being saved. Time must be given to those making decisions to be sure they understand what salvation is and how they are to be saved. It is not enough to fill out a card stating name and decision. Each one must understand the Lordship of Christ in his life. There must be an understanding of what sin is. There must be genuine repentance. Yes, there must be faith, but to "believe" without sorrowful repentance never leads to new life. After a clear understanding of how to be saved, each one seeking salvation should pray a simple prayer from his heart, asking Christ to forgive him and become his Savior and Lord. Anyone who is serious will be able to pray out loud. After each has prayed a sinner's prayer asking for salvation, he should be led to pray his first prayer as a new Christian—a prayer of thanksgiving.

No time in the life of the church is more important than the time of invitation. It should be prayerfully planned and carried out, expecting decisions.

Chapter 43

WHAT ARE THE ROLES OF THE PASTOR AND THE MEMBERS OF THE CHURCH?

How do the pastor and the members fit into God's plan for the church? First, let's look at God's plan for the church. Does God have an eternal plan for mankind which can be understood by His people? Definitely. The Bible clearly reveals what God has done in the past, gives us a picture of what He is doing now, and tells what He will do in the future.

We know that in the past mankind fell into sin and was separated from God. In an effort to draw man back to Himself, God used great men who related to Him by faith. Then He chose the Jewish nation and worked through it to demonstrate His love. God sent prophets to speak for Him. Finally God came to earth Himself in the person of his Son, Jesus. (John 1:14) Jesus preached repentance and forgiveness and men killed Him. In His death Jesus became the sacrifice, or payment, to set sinful men free—if they would by faith accept the sacrifice.

Once a person accepts Christ as his Savior and Lord he becomes a co-laborer with Christ, part of God's team destined to change the world.

The Bible says, *Those whom God had already chosen he also set apart to become like his Son, so that the Son would be the first among many brothers. And so those whom God set apart, he called; and those he called, he put right with himself, and he shared his glory with them.* Romans 8:29-30

Jesus spoke of the life of His followers when He said, *"Believe in the light, then, while you have it, so that you will be the people of light."* John 12:36

Christ established the church to be responsible for sharing the Good News.

Paul speaks of the eternal plan of God and the place of the church. *God, who is the Creator of all things, kept his secret hidden through all the past ages, in order that at the present time, by means of the church, the angelic rulers and powers in the heavenly world might learn of his wisdom in all its different forms. God did this according to his eternal purpose, which he achieved through Christ Jesus our Lord.* Ephesians 3:9-11

In all his wisdom and insight God did what he had purposed and made known to us the secret plan he had already decided to complete by means of Christ. This plan, which God will complete when the time is right, is to bring all creation together, everything in heaven and on earth, with Christ as head. All things are done according to God's plan and decision; and God chose us to be his own people in union with Christ because of his own purpose, based on what he had decided from the very beginning. Let us, then, who were the first to hope in Christ, praise God's glory! Ephesians 1:8-12

The church is to be victorious. Jesus said, *"I will build my church, and not even death will ever be able to overcome it."* Matthew 16:18

The New Testament church is made up of those who have been born again and have followed Christ in baptism. In Acts they are known as people of the Way. They are called believers. God has a clear plan of conquest for these people.

Paul speaks in Ephesians about the various gifts which God has given to His people—each church member. Every gift is to be used in building up the body, the church. The church is built up as it grows in spiritual maturity and as it adds new members. This is the expansion of God's Kingdom on earth today.

While in its earthly stage, the church will never be the dominant force, but its influence will be felt and it will become a threat to the forces of evil all over the earth. Christ is the head of this body and the source of its life, and He has definite plans for it.

Now back to the idea of various gifts given to members. These gifts are to be used for God in the expansion of His Kingdom.

The Bible says, *It was he who **gave gifts to mankind;** he appointed some to be apostles, others to be prophets, others to be evangelists, others to be pastors and teachers. He did this to prepare all God's people for the work of Christian service, in order to build up the body of Christ.* Ephesians 4:11-12

He gave various gifts of ministry. These gifts were meant to be used to build up the body of Christ.

What is the role of the pastor and the members in the development of the local church? What is the work of the pastor and what is the work of the church members in the expansion of the Kingdom of God?

We will look at two common views of ministry. First, the popular traditional view and second, the revolutionary Biblical view.

The **traditional view** became popular when the Christian religion was spreading throughout the Roman empire and caught the attention of Emperor Constantine. Constantine realized that it would be a good political move to join forces with the rapidly spreading religion. So he declared the pagan Roman empire to be

Christian. This diluted the church as paganism identified with Christianity.

This was the beginning of a thousand years of dark ages for the church. The Bible became a book for the educated clergy only. The common man was at the mercy of the clergy who told him what to believe. The church leaders were not to be questioned. Many of the religious leaders were not Christian in nature. The Roman church became more corrupt as it was led by corrupt religious leaders who came to be known as popes. A concept of ministry was being molded which has lasted to the twenty-first century—even in Protestant and evangelical churches. Ministry was for the professionals. The members simply followed. Power was in the hands of the clergy.

The Great Reformation of the sixteenth century brought some changes as Martin Luther declared that the Bible should be open to the common man and that anyone could pray directly to God. But much of the dark age mentality hangs on in the minds of religious leaders today. There is need for an extension of the Reformation so that, not only will man be able to enjoy the privilege of direct access to God, but also will accept the corresponding responsibility to minister.

The gap between the clergy and laity is still too great. God's people need to be set free to minister in meaningful ways in the world as well as in the church.

Many people are bored with a religion "attached" to their lives. Only when work and religion become related can God's eternal purpose have meaning. And only as a person is consciously a part of God's eternal plan will life be filled with direction and joy.

The traditional view of ministry may be better understood with the following illustration.

Traditional View of Ministry

| C H U R C H | supports program and work of pastor/staff — — — — —> attends — — — — —> tithes — — — — —> agrees | P A S T O R & Staff | witnesses — — — — —> visits sick — — — — —> wins the lost — — — — —> | W O R L D |

In this traditional concept of ministry, members are called "laity."

The work of the laity is to support the pastor as he does the ministry.

This support comes in three forms:
- Attend
- Tithe
- Agree

If a member does all of these he is a great member.

A layman is someone who is not trained or skilled. So he cannot be trusted with too much of the real ministry. He supports the pastor and the pastor's program.

In this concept of ministry, the "laymen" tend to be lazy, and rarely will they win someone to Christ. Usually the best they can do is take someone to The Minister.

The pastor is recognized as the professional minister.

He is called "Father," "Reverend," or "Pastor."

He is considered as The Minister.

When the layman finds someone who wants to be born again, he must go to The Minister to get help and direction.

Usually in this system, the pastor dominates the worship service, since he views the members as "only laymen."

The ego trip can be great for the pastor. He enjoys the titles and limelight.

The pastor is the only one at the front lines of battle in the world.

The pastor usually is not taken seriously by the world. He is "paid to do this," the people say.

The world is not won to Christ, and the pastor wears himself out in trying to do all the ministry.

Some pastors and members have grown tired of these roles of ministry and have gone to the New Testament seeking a more meaningful concept that will liberate the clergy and the laity.

Next we will look at the Biblical concept of ministry.

Biblical View of Ministry

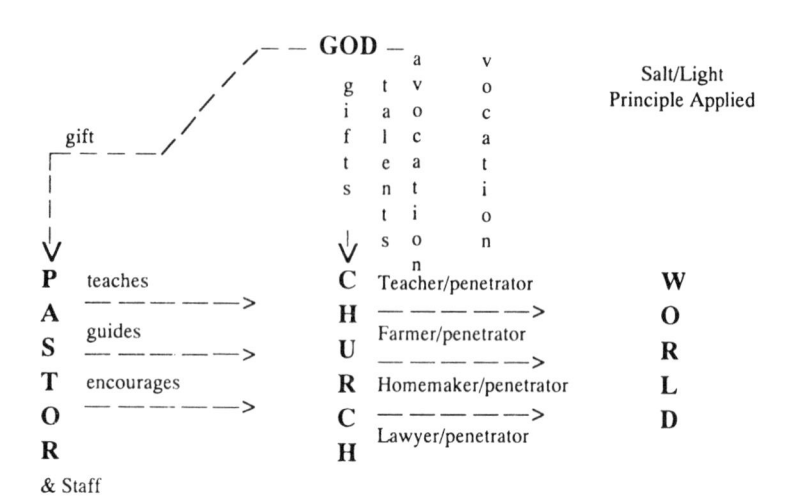

```
                    ┌ ─ ─ GOD ─ ┐
                 ╱              │   a      v             Salt/Light
               ╱             g  t   v      o          Principle Applied
             ╱               i  a   o      c
      gift ╱                 f  l   c      a
    ┌ ─ ─ ─                  t  e   a      t
    │                        s  n   t      i
    │                           t   i      o
    ↓                           s   o      n
    V                           ↓   n
    P    teaches                V
    A    ─ ─ ─ ─ ─>             C   Teacher/penetrator        W
    S    guides                 H   ─ ─ ─ ─ ─>                O
    T    ─ ─ ─ ─ ─>             U   Farmer/penetrator         R
    O    encourages             R   ─ ─ ─ ─ ─>                L
    R    ─ ─ ─ ─ ─>             C   Homemaker/penetrator      D
         & Staff                H   ─ ─ ─ ─ ─>
                                    Lawyer/penetrator
```

The pastor is the equipper. His primary work is to equip the members so they can minister in the world.	The members are trained, therefore not laymen. A new believer is a layman, but if he remains a layman for more than six months, the pastor and church should re-evaluate the programs of the church.	The world is where the members live.
He is a minister, not The Minister.		When sharing their faith, they are not seen as paid salesmen; they are known as satisfied customers.
A pastor must be out among the members so he can know the needs of the church body. This will enable him to properly feed them so they will be equipped to minister effectively.	A church with 100 members should expect to have 100 ministers (not pastors).	They are full-time ministers where they live and work.
	Members now find meaning to life in their church and work, properly relating their church/work life to God's eternal plan.	All levels of society are being penetrated.
The pastor is the player/coach. His work is more meaningful now that he is an equipper.	Their vocation is the same — world penetration, using their God-given talents as a means to reach the world for Christ.	
The pastor must be in the world doing various ministries, but his primary ministry is equipping the body.	God gives gifts to the members to minister to each other. These gifts include teaching, encouragement, sharing, prayer, and others, as the body needs.	

The pastor ministers to ministers so they can minister.

Chapter 44

WHAT DOES THE BIBLE SAY ABOUT DEACONS?

We will look at what the Bible says about this topic because some will be asking, "Should we have deacons in our church and should they be ordained?" Findley Edge, a prominent professor and author states in his book, *A Quest for Vitality in Religion,* "We give deacons a central responsibility in the life of our churches on the basis of a few verses of Scripture. Even the practice of ordination has limited references in Scripture." Many accept an elaborate system of the office of deacon assuming it is a Bible-based system. It is important to see what the Bible says about this subject.

The word "deacon" comes from the New Testament Greek word diakonos, which means servant. The word diakonos is sometimes translated into English as minister, helper, deacon, but most often servant. There are two Greek words for servant or slave. One is "doulos" which emphasizes personal allegiance to the master. The second word is "diakonos" which emphasizes service for the master. Paul used both words to describe himself. He was a servant (doulos, Titus 1:1) of Jesus Christ called to serve (diakonos, 1 Corinthians 3:5) the Gospel.

We will look at the various ways "diakonos" is used in the New Testament.

1. Diakonos is used to describe domestic servants. John 2:5,9

At the wedding feast in Cana, *Jesus' mother then told the servants* (diakonois), "*Do whatever he tells you."* v.5

2. Diakonos is used to describe civil rulers. Romans 13:4

193

Paul tells the believers to obey government authorities. He says, *...because he is God's servant* (diakonos) *working for your own good.*

3. Diakonos is used to describe the work of Christ. Romans 15:8

For I tell you that Christ's life of service (diakonon) *was on behalf of the Jews.*

4. Diakonos is used to describe the relationship of the followers of Christ to their Lord.

John 12:26 - *"Whoever wants to serve* (diakone) *me must follow me, so that my servant* (diakonas) *will be with me where I am."*

Ephesians 6:21 - *Tychicus, our dear brother and faithful servant* (diakonos) *in the Lord's work.*

Colossians 1:7 - *You learned of God's grace from Epaphras, our dear fellow servant* (diakonos), *who is Christ's faithful worker on our behalf.*

5. Diakonos is used to describe the followers of Christ in their relationship to each other.

Matthew 20:26-27 - *"If one of you wants to be great, he must be the servant* (diakonos) *of the rest; and if one of you wants to be first, he must be your slave."* (doulos)

Matthew 23:11 - *"The greatest one among you must be your servant."* (diakonos)

Mark 9:35 - *"Whoever wants to be first must place himself last of all and be the servant* (diakonos) *of all."*

Mark 10:43 - *"If one of you wants to be great, he must be the servant* (diakonos) *of the rest;"*

6. Diakonos is used to describe the servants of Christ as they preached the gospel.

1 Corinthians 3:5 - *After all, who is Apollos? And who is Paul? We are simply God's servants.* (diakonoi)

2 Corinthians 3:5-6 - Paul was speaking of himself as a servant when he said, *The capacity we have comes from God; it is he who made us capable of serving* (diakonous) *the new covenant...*

2 Corinthians 6:4 - *Instead, in everything we do we show that we are God's servants* (diakonoi) *by patiently enduring troubles...*

Ephesians 3:7 - *I was made a servant* (diakonos) *of the gospel by God's special gift, which he gave me...*

Colossians 1:23 - *It is of this gospel that I, Paul, became a servant...* (diakonos)

Colossians 1:25 - *And I have been made a servant* (diakonos) *of the church by God, who gave me this task...*

1 Timothy 4:6 - Paul speaking to Timothy, *If you give these instructions to the brothers, you will be a good servant* (diakonos) *of Christ Jesus...*

7. Diakonos is used to describe those who serve in the churches.

Romans 16:1 - *I recommend to you our sister Phoebe, who serves* (diakonon) *the church at Cenchreae.* Philippians 1:1 - *From Paul and Timothy, servants* (douloi) *of Christ Jesus—to all God's people in Philippi who are in union with Christ Jesus, including the church leaders and helpers.* (diakonois)

1 Timothy 3:8 - *Church helpers* (diakonous) *must also have a good character and be sincere...*

1 Timothy 3:12 - *A church helper* (diakonoi) *must have only one wife...*

Acts 6:1,4 - *The Greek-speaking Jews claimed that their widows were being neglected in the daily distribution* (diakonia) *of funds.* v.1 *...We ourselves, then, will give our full time* (service—diakonia) *to prayer and the work of preaching.* v.4 (Note that the same word is used to describe the service of waiting tables as the service of preaching—both were serving the Lord.)

8. Diakonos is used to describe false prophets—servants of Satan.

2 Corinthians 11:14-15 - *Even Satan can disguise himself to look like an angel of light! So it is no great thing if his servants* (diakonoi) *disguise themselves to look like servants of righteousness.*

Conclusion

The word diakonos is used in many different situations to describe someone who serves. The same root word is used for many different types of service. Many people believe that the traditional office of deaconship was established in Acts 6. The word deacon (diakonos) is not found in that chapter. The word diakonia, which describes a service rendered, is used two times, one referring to the seven men chosen to handle the financial problems and the other referring to the desire of the Apostles to give full time to preaching the Gospel. The same word describes both ministries.

The traditional role of a board of deacons as a ruling body in the church is definitely not Biblical. The work the men in Acts 6 were chosen for is like the work of a benevolence committee. Some of the above verses indicate that everyone who follows

Christ is a servant (deacon). All believers are to have an attitude of servanthood, always ready to minister when the need arises.

Various needs in the church family call for special attention. Often this special attention is best met by a group of believers. The group may be called a committee, board, or council. Some such committees found in churches today are: personnel committee, house and grounds committee, benevolence committee, music committee, evangelism committee, etc. All who serve (diakonos) on any of these committees should be faithful and godly people who are willing to share their faith. They should be set apart by the church and commissioned to serve. The commissioning or electing is not necessarily for the lifetime of the person, but for as long as the need exists and for as long as the church desires that person to serve in that position.

The most damaging aspect of the modern concept of a few deacons in a local church is the omission of the majority from being ministers. It is far more Biblical for a church of 100 members to have 100 ministers (servants, deacons), than for that church to have five deacons/servants. This does not mean that all will be pastors or leaders, but all will be full time ministers every day in their work and in the church. A deacon is a servant. A servant is a deacon. Every believer is called to be a servant. The kinds of service (diakonia) may vary, but if done in Christ's name, one is not greater than the other. One may wait tables (John 2:5,9 and Acts 6:1) and the other may preach the gospel (Acts 6:4), but both in God's eyes are His children using gifts which He has given to them.

Chapter 45

WHO SHOULD BE ALLOWED TO SPEAK TO THE CHURCH?

Should a preacher who is unknown to the members be allowed to stand in the pulpit? If a preacher just stops by to worship with the church, should he be asked to preach?

Normally, the pastor of the church has studied and prepared and God has given him a message for the church. If the message is from God, he will not quickly allow someone else to preach in his place. He will feel an urgency and a desire to share the message God has given him.

It is not necessarily a sign of courtesy when the pastor always invites a visiting preacher to preach. It may be a sign of laziness and lack of preparation and urgency on the part of the pastor.

If the visiting preacher is not well known by the pastor and people, he should not be invited to say anything.

Even if the visiting preacher is well known, it is not necessary that he be given an opportunity to speak. Often he is not prepared to speak and the church does not need for a man just to talk.

Beware of the visitor who asks to speak to the group. Unless the pastor and people know him well, his request should be gently but firmly turned down. Humility is not usually a strong characteristic of the person who makes a request to speak to the church.

There are people who are just looking for a place to talk. These people have no right to address the church. Valuable time will be wasted and the scheduled order of service will be disrupted. The person who wants to say something often will not know when to stop talking.

There are some people who would like an opportunity to speak to promote their philosophy or erroneous doctrine. The church must be aware of such people and not allow them an opportunity to stand before the congregation to speak.

There can be a danger in a church leader saying, "Does anyone want to say a word?" This is not wise if there are people present who are visitors. A member of a cult group would sometimes take advantage of such a situation.

A member should never take the initiative to invite a "friend" to preach without approval of the pastor and church.

In conclusion: Be very careful about who is allowed to speak to the church at any of the worship times or Bible studies.

Only those known to be sound in doctrine and morality should be allowed to stand in the pulpit.

Chapter 46

HOW DOES THE CHURCH RECEIVE NEW MEMBERS?

New members are usually added by baptism or by transfer from another church of the same belief and practice. We will look at both of these.

Receiving New Members By Baptism

The following steps are suggested:

1. Proper counseling is done to be as sure as possible that the person is really born again and has a new life style.

2. The person comes before the church during the worship service stating that he has been born again and desires to be baptized and become a member of the church.

3. The church recognizes the person as a candidate for baptism and membership.

4. The church may give the candidate an outline to help him in writing out his testimony. The candidate must be willing and able to write a clear testimony. A church member will help him to understand how to write out the testimony and how to give it orally.

5. Before the next worship service, the candidate should submit the written testimony to the church leader or some other designated person.

6. The candidate will give his testimony before the church, telling in detail about how, where, and when he was born again.

7. The candidate attends a new member class studying "I Have Been Born Again, What Next?" He must complete this orientation study or another which the church may decide to use.

The new member class can be held at any time convenient to the new candidate/s for membership. The church will elect the people to lead the new member orientation class. (If the church has additions on a regular basis, it may be helpful to have more than one new member class.)

8. During the weeks of the orientation class the church will have opportunity to observe the behavior of the candidate. Not only will his moral behavior be observed but also his faithful attendance in the activities of the church.

9. After the candidate has completed the orientation and has proven that he is really interested in being a part of the church family, his name will be presented to the church at a monthly business meeting. The church leader will recommend that the candidate be accepted for baptism and church membership.

(If the candidate has not been willing to give his testimony or attend the new member orientation, he should not be presented for acceptance by the church. The leader should report on the candidate, but postpone acceptance until the candidate shows that he is serious enough to comply with the requirements for membership.)

10. The church will vote to receive the person for baptism and membership.

11. When the candidate is baptized he becomes a member of the church.

Receiving New Members By Statement Or Transfer

Repeat all of the above steps except #10 and #11. Number ten is changed to read: The church will vote to receive the person for membership.

Members added by statement or transfer are people who are already baptized members of another church of the same belief and practice. For a person to be received in this manner, the church he comes from must have the same basic doctrines and practices as the church he is seeking to join.

For example, if a person comes from a church that baptizes babies or uses sprinkling instead of immersion, he does not qualify for membership by transfer or statement. If members come in with radically different doctrines, the result will be disunity within the church family and this cannot be allowed.

The church secretary should obtain the name and address of the church where the candidate is a member and write to the church informing them of this person's request for membership. It should be asked if he is a member of the church and if he is in good standing. Upon receipt of a letter of affirmation the person becomes a member of the church where he now attends. The other church will drop the person's name from their list of members.

Churches generally take much too lightly the receiving of new members. A healthy church must be strong and strict at the point of orientation and acceptance of new members.

Chapter 47

HOW SHOULD A BAPTISMAL SERVICE BE CONDUCTED?

Those being baptized should have met the requirements under Receiving New Members by Baptism on page 196.

Time For The Baptism

The church, in consultation with those to be baptized, will set the date for the baptismal service. The time should be when many of the members can attend.

Place For The Baptism

The baptism may be in a river, the sea, or any other body of water. Some churches have baptistries built into their church buildings. Some have a container made of concrete built outside. The water should be about waist deep and clean.

Atmosphere For The Baptism

While the baptismal service is one of great joy, order and reverence should be observed.

Instructions For Those To Be Baptized

Before the service begins, the one doing the baptizing should give brief instructions to those who are to be baptized. These instructions include at least the following:

- Hold knees stiff, back and neck rigid in an upright posture.
- Hold the hands across the breast.

As the person is being lowered into the water, he is to hold his breath for just a moment. A handkerchief will not be used to hold the nose. This is a picture of a dead person being buried.

Instructions For The One Doing The Baptizing

Stand to one side of the candidate, grasp the folded hands of the candidate with your left hand and say, "Have you, _____, accepted Jesus Christ as your personal Savior and Lord?" The candidate will answer, "Yes I have." The minister then will say, "Because you have accepted Christ as your Savior and Lord, and because He commands that you be baptized, I baptize you, my brother/sister in the name of the Father and of the Son and of the Holy Spirit. Amen."

The minister places his right hand on the back of the candidate's neck and gently and slowly lowers the candidate into the water. The head should be placed just under the water and raised back out immediately. There should not be splashing of the water.

The Baptismal Service

This will vary, depending upon where the baptismal service is held. If at the church house, it may be a part of a regular worship service. Normally, when held as a part of the worship service, there will be a sermon before the baptism. The sermon may relate to the topic of baptism. If the service is held at the sea or river, the following order may be followed:

1. A brief explanation by the leader concerning the meaning of baptism.

2. Scripture reading. Some appropriate Scriptures are Matthew 3:1-17 and Acts 8:26-39.

3. Singing

4. Prayer

5. The leader will go into the water, followed by the candidates.

6. After all are baptized, the group may want to join hands and sing an appropriate hymn.

7. Closing prayer

Those who were baptized are now officially members of the church.

The church may give baptismal certificates at the next worship service.

Note: Some people may ask the question, "What do we do if we have no pastor? Who will do the baptizing?" The answer to this is the same as for observing the Lord's Supper. Anyone authorized by the church may conduct the baptismal service.

"Does he have to be 'ordained' before he can baptize or lead in the Lord's Supper?" The answer is no.

"Must a person have seminary training before he can baptize?" Again the answer is no.

ALERT:
The one leading the baptismal service should meet the basic qualifications of a church leader found in I Timothy 3:1-13. The church must be careful in choosing who is allowed to lead the baptismal service or the Lord's Supper.

Chapter 48

HOW DOES A CHURCH OBSERVE THE LORD'S SUPPER?

The church will decide how often the Lord's Supper (Communion) will be observed. Jesus said, "As often as you do this, do it in memory of me." Some churches observe the Supper once a month. Others have felt it best to have it once every three months.

When a church has the Lord's Supper every Sunday or every month, it can become like an ordinary service and lose some of its special meaning. If the Supper is observed quarterly, it will be central rather than simply attached to a regular worship service.

The Lord's Supper is a memorial service—a time of remembering the death of Christ on the cross. The two elements used in the Lord's Supper, the bread and juice, are symbols of Jesus' broken body and shed blood.

The observance of the Lord's Supper is a solemn and sacred time. It should be held in a spirit of reverence and worship. Quietness and meditation should fill the place where the service is being held.

PREPARATION FOR THE LORD'S SUPPER

Who should lead the service?

It usually is the pastor, but anyone the church authorizes may lead the service. The one leading and those helping should be members in good standing with the church. They should be respected and godly people. It is not necessary that the leader be ordained or have special schooling.

What preparations need to be made before the service?

The leader must see that proper arrangements are made. There should be a small table at the front of the meeting place where the juice and bread can be placed.

The leader must see that someone is responsible for purchasing and preparing the juice and bread.

The leader must see that everything is prepared and in place before the people arrive for the memorial service.

The leader must know what he is going to do in the memorial service before it begins. He should know who is going to help serve the Lord's Supper. It is well if together they review each step of the service beforehand so they will know what to do and will have a relaxed confidence.

Who will help the leader?

It depends on the size of the congregation. If the church is small, two people may be enough. These two will distribute the bread and juice to the people. They also may lead in prayer before the bread and juice are distributed.

What are the elements to be used in the Lord's Supper?

Bread - Bread without leavening is traditionally used because Jesus instituted the Lord's Supper at a Passover meal. Unleavened bread was used for this meal.

Many churches use ordinary crackers. If these are used they should be broken into small pieces and placed on a plate. Some churches buy bread especially prepared for use in the Lord's Supper. This is already broken and ready for use. It can be bought at some Christian book stores.

Wine - Most churches use grape juice, which is the fruit of the vine. This can be purchased at most grocery stores.

How to prepare the bread and juice.

The bread should be broken into small pieces no larger than a half inch in diameter and placed on a plate. Be sure to prepare a little more than is needed.

The juice should be poured into very small glasses. These glasses can be purchased at many Christian book stores. They will be used for many years by the church. If "communion glasses" cannot be obtained, very small ordinary glasses can be used with only a small amount of juice in each. Be sure to prepare more than is needed.

The church will provide the elements used.

The elements should be obtained at least a day before the memorial supper and should be prepared before the hour of the service. The table should be prepared with the elements placed on it before anyone arrives for the service.

A cloth should be used to cover the elements and the table. This cloth is not removed until the leader is ready to distribute the elements to the people.

THE OBSERVANCE OF THE LORD'S SUPPER

A sermon related to the Lord's Supper may be given as the first part of the memorial service.

The leader should state the meaning of the Lord's Supper at the beginning of the service. He should state who may partake and those who should not. This should be done in a way that will not offend people. The Supper is for baptized believers.

The following is an order of service which may be used.

Church Member: Scripture reading - Luke 22:7-20

Pastor says: We will now observe the Lord's Supper. This memorial supper was given to us to celebrate in memory of Jesus' broken body and shed blood.

(Helpers will come to the front and stand beside the table.)

Pastor says: The Bible tells us that on the night before Jesus was betrayed, at the conclusion of the Passover which he and his disciples were celebrating, He took bread and blessed it, broke it, and gave it to his disciples and said, *"This is my body, which is given for you."*

One of the helpers will lead in prayer.

The pastor gives the plate to the helpers for distribution to the congregation.

Pastor says: Please hold the bread until all have been served. (This will need to be said only until the members have learned the procedure.)

After all have been served, the helpers return to the memorial table. The pastor will serve the helpers and then the helpers will serve the pastor.

The pastor takes a piece of bread and holds it up where all members can see it.

Pastor says: *"This, then, is the bread that came down from heaven; it is not like the bread that your ancestors ate, but then later died. The one who eats this bread will live forever."* John 6:58

The pastor eats the bread and the people do the same.

Pastor says: On that same night Jesus took the cup and blessed it, gave it to his disciples and said, "*This is my blood which was shed for you.*"

One of the helpers will lead in prayer.

The pastor hands the juice to the helpers for distribution.

Following the distribution, the helpers return to the memorial table.

The pastor serves the helpers and then the helpers serve the pastor.

Pastor says: *Indeed, according to the Law almost everything is purified by blood, and sins are forgiven only if blood is poured out.* Hebrews 9:22

But if we live in the light—just as he is in the light—then we have fellowship with one another, and the blood of Jesus, his Son, purifies us from every sin. 1 John 1:7

The pastor then leads the congregation in drinking the cup.

Pastor says: *This means that every time you eat this bread and drink from this cup you proclaim the Lord's death until he comes.* 1 Corinthians 11:26

Pastor says: After Jesus and his disciples ate the bread and drank the wine, the Bible says they sang a hymn and went out. Let us prayerfully sing _____ as we depart. May God bless each of you.

Chapter 49

HOW SHOULD A DEDICATION SERVICE FOR A CHILD BE CONDUCTED?

Baby dedication is not to be confused with baby baptism. Bible believers will not have their babies "baptized" because it is not taught in the Bible. It is against Bible teachings concerning baptism. Baptism never brings salvation to anyone, child or adult. Salvation comes only after a person repents of sin and exercises a conscious faith in Christ as his Savior and Lord. Some churches do not have dedication services for children because they fear it may be misinterpreted as something similar to baby baptism.

It is good for parents to dedicate their children to God. Parents who do not desire to have a public dedication should privately dedicate their child to God.

What does it mean for parents to dedicate their child to God?

It is a time when parents consciously give their child and its future to God. They are acknowledging that they want God to use this child for His glory.

It is a time when parents make known publicly that they will do their best to see that their child is led to know and love the Lord through a study of the Scriptures.

They are stating publicly that they will see to it that their child faithfully attends a church that teaches the Word of God.

They are stating that they will personally live in such a way that their child will see Christ in their daily lives.

The time of dedication is a time when parents dedicate themselves to raise their child in a godly, Bible-believing home.

What is the Biblical basis of the dedication service?

In I Samuel we read about a godly woman who prayed for God to give her a son. After God answered her prayer, she dedicated her son to the Lord. The Scripture says: "*If you give me a son, I promise that I will dedicate him to you for his whole life*"... *So it was that she became pregnant and gave birth to a son. She named him Samuel, and explained, "I asked the Lord for him." ...She took Samuel, young as he was, to the house of the Lord...* 1 Samuel 1:11,20,24 At the house of the Lord she said, "*I asked him for this child, and he gave me what I asked for. So I am dedicating him to the Lord. As long as he lives, he will belong to the Lord.*" *Then they worshipped the Lord there.* 1 Samuel 1:27-28

The Bible says in Deuteronomy 6:5-7, *Love the Lord your God with all your heart, with all your soul, and with all your strength. Never forget these commands that I am giving you today. Teach them to your children. Repeat them when you are at home and when you are away, when you are resting and when you are working.*

Paul wrote to Timothy these words found in 2 Timothy 3:14-17, *But as for you, continue in the truths that you were taught and firmly believe. You know who your teachers were, and you remember that ever since you were a child, you have known the Holy Scriptures, which are able to give you the wisdom that leads to salvation through faith in Christ Jesus. All Scripture is inspired by God and is useful for teaching the truth, rebuking error, correcting faults, and giving instruction for right living, so that the person who serves God may be fully qualified and equipped to do every kind of good deed.*

You will note that the Bible is for children as well as adults. It is natural for true believers to desire with all their hearts to provide every opportunity possible for their children to learn the message of the Bible.

The Bible says, *Parents, do not treat your children in such a way as to make them angry. Instead, raise them with Christian discipline and instruction.* Ephesians 6:4

This is the promise being made by the parents at the dedication service—to raise their children with Christian discipline and instruction.

From previously given Bible verses, it is clear that there is one reliable book for religious instruction and discipline—the Word of God, the Bible. No other book can become a substitute for the Bible.

Love is a major theme of the Bible. Anyone who has experienced the New Birth will want the best for their children, and the way of the Bible is the best way, and it is the only way that leads to heaven. Because of love, parents who have been born again want their child to enjoy the same peace, joy and purpose in life that they have experienced.

When should the child be dedicated?

This can be done at any time convenient for the parents. Many choose to have the dedication when the child is one or two months old.

The service is often a part of a regular worship service. It can be at the beginning or at the end. It is a very serious matter and should be observed with deep reverence.

Who should lead the dedication service?

Usually the pastor will lead the service. If the church does not have a pastor, a church member may be chosen to lead. The worship leader can do this very effectively. One need not be "ordained" or have special education to qualify to lead the dedication service. The person should be well respected and committed to the Lord.

How is the service to be conducted?

1. The parents and the child are invited to sit at the front.

2. The leader explains the purpose of the dedication. He will explain that it does not bring salvation to the child.

3. Some or all of the Scriptures in this lesson may be read.

4. The parents are asked to stand at the front, facing the leader. They will be holding the child.

5. **The leader may say to the parents,**

    "Before God and all these witnesses, do you promise, with God's help, to bring up little _____(name) in the way of the Lord?"

    Parents answer: We do.

    Leader says:

    "Do you promise to make it possible for _____(name) to learn the Word of God through Bible study in your home and through the opportunities offered by the church?"

    Parents answer: We do.

Leader: Leads in a dedication prayer for the parents and the child.

Leader: Presents a dedication certificate to the parents. (The giving of a certificate is optional. Certificates can be purchased at most Christian book stores.)

The service is concluded with members greeting the parents and wishing them well.

Chapter 50

WHAT SHOULD WE DO WHEN THERE IS AN EMERGENCY NEED IN ONE OF THE CHURCH FAMILIES?

Examples of such needs are:

1. A family does not have enough money to buy medicine for a sick child.

2. A family has a death and there are extra expenses which the family cannot bear.

3. The house of one of the families burns.

4. A storm badly damages the house of a member.

5. Non-church members come to the pastor for financial assistance.

6. Beggars or swindlers come to the pastor or members telling long stories of financial problems and asking for help.

People often go to the pastor thinking that he can easily get money for them. (The pastor does not have access to the church's money.)

The pastor does not have money to give to meet everyone's needs. If he gives to one church member but cannot give to another, he may be criticized by the people for playing favorites.

Sometimes there are a few families in the church who may appear to have more money than others and people make it a habit to seek these families out in times of crisis. This puts an unfair burden on these families.

What is the church to do? Are they to turn their backs on everyone and refuse to help? This is not the Christian attitude toward people in need. There should be a system which is workable for the church family and which is fair for all.

Consider the following:

First, church members must recognize that when they join the group they become part of a family. Membership in the family carries with it certain privileges and responsibilities.

When one member of the family hurts, the whole family should be aware of it and feel a responsibility to help when needed.

The church family loves members of the body and will show it, especially in times of great need.

The crisis or emergency of one family is not the sole responsibility of the pastor or one of the families of the church. It is the responsibility of the whole body, the church.

The person who is really a child of God will be slow to ask for help. God's people have a sense of dignity unknown to those not born again. People should do their very best to meet their own needs from within their immediate family. This is where responsibility begins. If needs cannot be met by the biological family, then a person may want to go to the larger family, the church. It is true that the church family should be sensitive enough to needs within the membership that the church would take the initiative and not require that a member come asking for help.

A suggested system to help the church meet needs is as follows:

1. Elect a benevolence committee.

This could be done at the regular annual election of church officers, teachers, committees, etc. The committee would serve for one year like most other committees, with a new committee being elected each year. (If the church has a Constitution and By-laws, this committee would fall within its guide lines on committees.)

The committee could have 3-5 members. Committee members should be faithful in the activities of the church. They should be wise and spiritually mature. It may be best if the pastor is not a member of this committee.

2. Everyone seeking assistance must meet with this committee before the need is presented to the church.

3. The committee will not have authority to grant the request of anyone seeking help. They should hear the needs as presented by the person or family. After a careful and prayerful study of the request, the committee should then make their recommendation to the church, either at a regular business meeting or at a special called meeting of the members.

4. The church, upon hearing the recommendation of the benevolence committee, will make the final decision. The church is not obligated to follow the recommendation of the committee.

When the committee reports to the church, those seeking help may be present at the beginning when their request is presented. But there should be a period when they are asked to leave so the members can discuss more openly the request and make the final decision without the requesting family present.

5. There may be some requests that will not need to be presented to the entire church. The committee does not need to present requests which they are sure are from false needs or from professional beggars, etc.

This simple system makes it easier for the church to be a loving family, helping those who really need help.

This allows for all the church to participate in helping those in need. The money to meet the needs will come from the church funds or from a special love offering given by the members.

This removes from the pastor the burden of deciding who should be helped, how much to give, and where to find the resources.

What is the pastor to do when someone comes to him asking for financial assistance? He should be instructed by the church to refer such requests to the benevolence committee.

The pastor should not by-pass the committee and take the request directly to the church.

The responsibility of this committee should be well known by all the church members.

All church members should be well aware of the steps necessary to obtain special assistance in times of crisis or emergency.

Chapter 51

HOW DOES A CHURCH DISCIPLINE MEMBERS?

First we must understand the meaning of the word discipline. We often think of discipline only as corrective, and usually involving punishment. This is only one part of discipline. We will look at two aspects of discipline, developmental and correctional.

DEVELOPMENTAL DISCIPLINE

"Discipline" and "disciple" come from the same root word. It means to teach, to lead, to guide. Every church must be involved in this kind of discipline. All of the programs of the church should be involved in the disciplining or discipling of members. Developmental discipline helps believers to know the relationship between their daily living and the purpose of God, and seeks to equip them to carry out that purpose. Jesus spoke of discipline when he said to his disciples, *"Go, then, to all peoples everywhere and make them my disciples: baptize them in the name of the Father, the Son, and the Holy Spirit, and teach them to obey everything I have commanded you. And I will be with you always, to the end of the age."* Matthew 28:19-20

Corrective discipline will not be needed as often when a church takes seriously its task of developmental discipline. A church has the responsibility to provide organizational structures and programs which will give every member the opportunity to develop into a productive Christian. If a member refuses to grow through participation in the fellowship and teaching programs of the church, he needs special attention and encouragement. This act of encouragement becomes part of developmental discipline.

Many churches are concerned about all those who have "gone astray" into sin, who have completely dropped out of the church life. Most churches are not doing much to reach these people. The best way to prevent the going astray of members is to have a vital, relevant program of training which begins the day a person comes into the church as a new member. This means that the starting point of developmental discipline should be a well-planned new member class. Two or three weeks for this class is not adequate. Some suggest that two to twelve months of special training should be given to the new member. (This does not mean, of course, that the new member will not immediately become involved in the regular activities of the church.)

Having only a one hour worship service each week is not taking developmental discipline seriously. People need to have additional Bible study, prayer time, and fellowship with other believers.

CORRECTIVE DISCIPLINE

By corrective discipline we mean correcting, setting right, lifting up someone who has fallen. It is always to be redemptive and helpful. It is never to be done in anger, to get revenge, or to hurt. Correction is often painful but necessary in loving Christian relationships. The church that loves will correct members who fall into sin.

Why does a church not practice corrective discipline?

1. Because of a lack of concern.
2. Because the church does not recognize its significance as a body being made in the image of its head, Jesus.
3. Because it might hurt feelings.
4. Because "everyone is a sinner and who are we to cast a stone?"
5. Because of not knowing that it is the responsibility of the church.

In the New Testament there are three areas that call for corrective discipline. These are: sinning against a brother, immorality, and false teachings.

Sin Against a Brother - Matthew 18:15-17

In this passage Jesus tells what a Christian is to do when a Christian brother sins against him. He is to go to the brother and try to make things right. If the brother will not listen to him, he is to take one or two other members with him and try again to work things out with the brother. If the brother listens and there is understanding, forgiveness, and love, then all are blessed and happy. If the brother will not listen, he is to be treated as a "pagan."

How are we to treat a "pagan?" We are to love and pray for him, seeking to bring reconciliation.

Immorality - 1 Corinthians 5:1-13; 2 Corinthians 2:4-11

There was a problem of immorality in the church at Corinth. A member of the church was sleeping with his father's wife. Paul was very disturbed about the fact that the church had not taken any action. He scolded the church for being proud, yet living like the heathen.

From this passage we learn several things about corrective discipline.

1. The sin of immorality is disruptive in a church.

2. Paul did not have to think twice before coming to a conclusion that the erring man should be dealt with.

3. The purity of the body—the church, must be safe-guarded. In verses 6-7, Paul speaks of the deadening influence of sin—it is as

yeast in a batch of dough. He said, "You must remove the old yeast of sin so that you will be entirely pure."

4. In verse 13, Paul says, *"Remove the evil man from your group."* This indicates excommunication from the body. Can this be done with the hope of final redemption? Yes, it can be. In verse 5, Paul says, *You are to hand this man over to Satan for his body to be destroyed, so that his spirit may be saved in the Day of the Lord.* Paul is saying that discipline is necessary for two reasons: one for the welfare of the man himself, and second, for the welfare of the church.

5. It is a very serious church problem for a church member to live in open immorality of such magnitude that the basic institution of marriage and family life is threatened. To preserve the witness or reputation of the church is more important than retaining the physical presence of such a defiant, rebellious member.

What about a church member who has a mistress on the side? What about a pastor who has a girlfriend or even a second wife? What about a church member who gives himself to a life of sin?

Any of the examples above should be dealt with immediately. Without delay the erring church member should be suspended from any leadership position in the church. He should not be allowed to participate in privileges of membership such as voting and partaking of the Lord's Supper.

Any erring church member should have a chance to repent and change. A new life of opportunity may await those who repent and show over a period of time that their lives have changed. When repentance is genuine and there is an obvious change in conduct, the privileges of membership should be restored to the person.

Note 2 Corinthians 2:4-11. Here we see the love and redemptive aspect of corrective discipline. Paul believed that forgiveness should be extended to anyone who repents. The seeming harsh treatment of suspension and taking away all rights as participants in the church is meant to lead to lifting up and helping a fallen brother. This is love. To have a pastor or member live in open sexual immorality and treat it as a light matter is not demonstrating love. There will be times when members fall into sin, but it has not yet become a continuous pattern of life. This person will need to be helped, but suspension from duties and privileges may not be needed. This may be considered as preventive discipline. Early help may prevent the development of a pattern of habitual sin.

False Teachings - 1 Timothy 6:3-5; 2 John 9-11

In 1 Timothy, Paul warns Timothy about fellowship with those who teach false doctrines or who like to argue and philosophize.

In 2 John, John gives warning about fellowshipping with someone whose doctrine is different from the teachings of Christ.

From these passages we understand that a person should not be allowed to fellowship with a church if he insists on teaching false doctrines. A brother in the church who begins to teach false doctrines should be corrected by the church. It is not with a spirit of pride of self-righteousness that this correction is made, but out of loving humility.

A church can begin to deal with corrective discipline by electing a personnel committee.

The church should elect a personnel committee at the annual election of officers and teachers. This committee will be responsible for seeking solutions to problems within the membership such as has been given in this lesson.

This committee must be made up of mature Christians.
It is important that committee members not be gossipers. They must be able to keep a secret which is not to be shared even with their mates. Whether rumor or fact, people's problems are not to be freely talked about.

The committee may have 3-5 members.

The pastor should not be a member of the committee.

Any news of serious sin among the members (fact or rumor) should be reported to this committee and the committee will prayerfully and quietly look into the matter.

If there is indeed a serious problem, the committee will talk to those involved and try to help resolve the problem. If it is a serious problem, the committee will need to bring a report and recommendation to the church.

The committee will not have power beyond counseling and recommending. Any disciplinary action must be done by the church and only after proper hearings and counseling.

Conclusion

Every church should reevaluate the use of discipline within its body.

Every church should ask:

Do we have a positive, developmental discipline that trains and teaches all our members to participate in God's program of world redemption? How can we do better in teaching our people? What new programs do we need to add? What are we doing that should be eliminated?

Do we love enough to apply corrective discipline when it is needed? Are we willing to correct a fallen member, even if he gives much money to the church? Do we have a high enough opinion of the nature of the church—so much that we will want to keep it as pure as possible?

The church that loves will practice discipline for the sake of its own witness, for the sake of individual lives in the church, for the sake of the lost world, and for the sake of bringing glory to Christ.

Chapter 52

HOW CAN A CHURCH ENCOURAGE MEMBERS TO STUDY THE BIBLE?

First, church leaders must be setting an example that reveals a regular, fruitful, and joyful Bible reading program. Anyone who believes the Bible to be the Word of God will find excitement and challenge when reading it. This excitement will be contagious. Church members will be aware of it. A church leader should be determined to read the Bible through each year. Most church members need to be encouraged to be consistent in reading the Bible.

Even though church members may be challenged to begin a Bible reading program, they need something to help them remain faithful. It is natural for a person to begin something with excitement and after a while lose that excitement. It is often like this with Bible reading. **Accountability** is important in all a person does. Our course of action is usually influenced when we are accountable to someone.

Some churches have a Bible reading report time. This is a time when members are accountable to the group for their Bible reading. The size of the church will make a difference in how this is done. A small church may have Bible reading report time before the worship hour, either on Sunday morning or Sunday night. Some may prefer another special time. If the church is large, it may be necessary to divide into small groups. An hour or more could be used in this time of sharing.

This is not a time of preaching, lecturing, or sharing ones own ideas, but a time to share directly from the Bible great verses that have spoken to the person that week. It will be important for you to read the third chapter in this book entitled, "How should I study the Bible?" The system of Bible study described in that lesson is easy to use with an accountability system such as this.

The Bible reading report time is more than a system of accountability. It is much more than checking up on each other. It is sharing with others. It is a method of teaching each other.

Some may say, "Isn't it boring to do this, just to read God's Word?" It depends on what a person thinks of God's Word. For His child it should never be boring. What God's Word says is much more exciting and important than what any man or woman says about God's Word. Paul said, *Until I come, give your time and effort to the public reading of the Scriptures and to preaching and teaching.* 1 Timothy 4:13 Note that Paul speaks of three activities—public reading, preaching, and teaching.

In the Old Testament we read how Ezra read the Word of God to the people. *So Ezra brought it to the place where the people had gathered—men, women, and the children who were old enough to understand. There in the square by the gate he read the Law to them from dawn until noon, and they all listened attentively. ...When the people heard what the Law required, they were so moved that they began to cry...So all the people went home and ate and drank joyfully and shared what they had with others, because they understood what had been read to them.* Nehemiah 8:2-3,9,12

Of another occasion we read, *For about three hours the Law of the Lord their God was read to them, and for the next three hours they confessed their sins and worshipped the Lord their God.* Nehemiah 9:3

In the local church it should be assumed that every member will be involved in daily Bible reading. Therefore, every member should be expected to participate in the report time.

There is nothing more important than for each church member to stay faithfully in the Word of God. The Holy Spirit will be the teacher and guide as the believer reads and studies. Of all books, the Bible is The Book. Those who read it will be changed. There is nothing more important than for a church leader to lead "his people" to rest in fields of green grass and to lead them to quiet pools of fresh water. (Psalm 23) It is the Word that nourishes and refreshes the believer.